The Lord My Portion

The Lord My Portion

(A Daily Devotional)

WATCHMAN NEE

Christian Fellowship Publishers, Inc.
New York

ISBN 0-935008-61-6

Available from the Publishers at:

11515 Allecingie Parkway
Richmond, Virginia 23235

Printed in the United States of America

PREFACE

"The Lord is my portion." So said the psalmist (Ps. 119.57 NASV) and Jeremiah (Lam. 3.24), and in so saying, they declare that their portion in life is none other than the Lord himself. The New Testament expresses the same thing, when Paul tells how Christ "was made unto us wisdom from God, both righteousness and sanctification and redemption" (1 Cor. 1.30 mg.). That Christ Jesus is now the portion of His people is a fact which lies at the heart of the gospel, and our discovery of this fact makes His grace and presence to become real to us.

The daily readings found in this devotional have been taken from the most recent publications of Watchman Nee. Although they cover a number of different topics, they seem to contain a call to us to know and experience Christ as our portion—as our all. It is with the hope that God's people may be helped to know the Lord as their daily portion that this book has been prepared.

The scripture quotations are from the American Standard Version of the Bible (1901), unless otherwise indicated.

CHRISTIAN FELLOWSHIP PUBLISHERS

JANUARY 1st

And after these things he went forth, and beheld a publican, named Levi, sitting at the place of toll, and said unto him, Follow me. And he forsook all, and rose up and followed him. Luke 5.27, 28.

Once when the Lord traveled and came to a certain place, He saw Matthew (Levi) sitting at the customs. He called Levi, saying, "Follow me," and the latter arose and followed the Lord. Suppose a stranger would say to us, "Follow me"; would we rise up and follow him? Certainly not. But here is a Man to whom Matthew is drawn as iron to a magnet; he cannot help but forsake his former life, wealth and all, and follow Him. Who knows the power behind Jesus' word that causes Matthew to renounce his sinful life and abandon everything? Here is a Man that whoever sees Him must repent and be saved, that whoever listens to His voice will receive a new life, that whoever hears His call will rise up and follow Him.

JANUARY 2nd

That the God of our Lord Jesus Christ, the Father of glory, may give unto you a spirit of wisdom and revelation in the knowledge of him. Ephesians 1.17.

If we truly know God we will not be disturbed even though there may come our way many questions. People may attempt to prove this or that thing, but we Christians can prove one very important thing—that God is indeed God and that we know Him who is so real. And by knowing Him, all problems are solved. Such knowledge does not rely on how logical are the reasons or how clear the doctrines; it relies only on revelation. How such revelation is absolutely necessary. We must ask God to give us the spirit of revelation so that we may really know Him. And knowledge such as this is the foundation of a believer and is of utmost importance.

JANUARY 3rd

Whereby he hath granted unto us his precious and exceeding great promises; that through these ye may become partakers of the divine nature. 2 Peter 1.4.

At a certain place there were a few sisters who usually asked God at the beginning of each year for a promise as to their annual report. One sister was of the anxious type. She became frightened whenever she thought of the past and looked forward to the future. She told the Lord of her actual condition. Consequently she received a promise from the Lord, saying, "Fear thou not, for I am with thee; be not dismayed, for I am thy God; I will strengthen thee; yea, I will help thee; yea, I will uphold thee with the right hand of my righteousness" (Is. 41.10). The six I's and my's and the three will's in this passage caused her to bow her head and worship God. She was moved to tears of joy and touched by the fullness of promises. Thereafter, whenever she was faced with difficulty or temptation she would read this word to herself as well as to God. Thus was she strengthened, helped and sustained through many years.

JANUARY 4th

The night is far spent, and the day is at hand: let us therefore cast off the works of darkness, and let us put on the armor of light. Romans 13.12.

Christ as the light of the world has already departed from this world. From the time of His ascension to the time of His coming again, the history of the world is but one long dark night. According to man's view the world is becoming better and brighter; but according to the word of God "the night is far spent" (Rom. 13.12).

We are now in that dark night, and hence can sense darkness all around. Are you aware of the darkness around you? If we walk in the light and live close to God by abiding in Christ, constantly judging the works of the flesh and obeying the leading of the Holy Spirit, we will most naturally perceive that this is truly a dark world.

JANUARY 5th

I am . . . the Living one; and I was dead, and behold, I am alive for evermore. Revelation 1.17, 18.

Apart from resurrection there is no life. At the time of the Garden of Eden man could see the tree of life, but today life is only found in resurrection since death has already come in. Life today is represented by resurrection. And hence, without resurrection no one may approach God. The life in us which we believers know today has passed through death, therefore it is called resurrection life. How exquisite is the word of Revelation: "I was dead, and behold, I am alive for evermore." Today's problem is no longer how to keep alive but how to be raised from among the dead. And just as our Lord is now standing on resurrection ground, so we too must stand on the same ground. Nothing but what stands on resurrection ground may come before God. Everything must go through death and be made alive again.

JANUARY 6th

And she called his name Moses, and said, Because I drew him out of the water. Exodus 2.10.

Three months after he was born, Moses was placed in the water. He was later pulled out of the water by the daughter of Pharaoh who adopted him as her son. Hence the name was give to him of "Moses"—which means "the drawing out of water." He was the first one drawn out. Later on the multitudes of the children of Israel would follow in his train by being drawn out themselves (the Red Sea experience). In the wilderness God dealt with Moses first, and then in the same wilderness He dealt with the children of Israel after they had been led out of Egypt by Moses. Unless *we* are delivered, we cannot expect *other* people to be delivered. If *we* do not have vision, how can we expect *others* to see God's way? Today God wishes to deal with us first. And after He has gotten some of us, we can then expect to gain other people.

JANUARY 7th

Come unto me, all ye that labor and are heavy laden.
Matthew 11.28.

Once I went to a village to preach, and there I learned the lesson of being heavy laden. The village I visited was on the other side of a hill, and was inaccessible by train or steamboat. I therefore took a steamboat to a certain point and from there walked uphill and then down to reach it. I carried with me many gospel booklets, pamphlets, some food and extra clothing. I felt fine with the first twenty steps, but afterward I could hardly bear the burden. I thought if I could only arrive at my destination quickly I then could rest. But there was no tree on the hill to shade me from the hot sun. And at that moment I began to understand how sinners must labor and how they must be heavy laden. Some of you may not have yet believed in the Lord Jesus; you therefore have no rest. Where, then, are you headed? Listen to the words of the Lord Jesus: "Come unto me, all ye that labor and are heavy laden, and I will give you rest."

JANUARY 8th

For ye received not the spirit of bondage again unto fear; but ye received the spirit of adoption, whereby we cry, Abba, Father. Romans 8.15.

After a person has accepted the Lord we say he not only is saved but also has been regenerated. This means that this man is now born of God. He has received a new life from Him. Having the life of God, a person is not only, negatively speaking, aware of sins but he also, positively speaking, knows God: for what we receive is not the spirit of a bond-slave but the spirit of sonship. We just naturally feel that God is very approachable and that calling Him "Abba, Father" is most sweet. The Holy Spirit bears witness with our spirit that we are children of God (Rom. 8.16). Knowing God as Father is therefore the inner consciousness of this life.

JANUARY 9th

Verily I say unto you, What things soever ye shall bind on earth shall be bound in heaven; and what things soever ye shall loose on earth shall be loosed in heaven.
Matthew 18.18.

We are most familiar with this word of our Lord, yet it should be realized that this word has reference to prayer. Here is clearly stated the relationship between prayer and God's work. God in heaven will only bind and loose what His children on earth have bound and loosed. Many things there are which need to be bound, but God will not bind them by himself alone. He wants His people to bind them on earth first, and then He will bind them in heaven. Many things are there also which should be loosed; but again, God is not willing to loose them alone: He waits until His people loose them on earth and then He will loose them in heaven. Think of it! All the actions in heaven are governed by the actions on earth! And likewise, all the movements in heaven are restricted by the movements on earth! God takes great delight in putting all His own works under the control of His people.

JANUARY 10th

*And I will make an everlasting covenant with them, that
I will not turn away from following them, to do them
good.* Jeremiah 32.40.

What does a covenant mean? A covenant speaks of
faithfulness, justice and law. If we make a covenant with
people, stipulating in it all the things that we will do, we will
be breaking our word and be faithless in case we do not perform according to this agreement.

In making covenant with man God condescends himself
to be bound and restricted by an agreement. He is willing
to forfeit His liberty in the covenant in order to facilitate
our possessing what He wants us to possess. The Most
High God, the Creator of the heavens and the earth, stoops
to make covenant with man. Such grace is beyond comparison. We can only bow and worship before the God of grace.

JANUARY 11th

*Put on the whole armor of God, that ye may be able to
stand against the wiles of the devil.* Ephesians 6.11.

Let us not forget that this spiritual armor is given
to the church and not to anyone individually. It requires the
church to deal with the enemy. What you as an individual
cannot see and safeguard, other members see and guard
against. Satan is not afraid of your personal prayer, but he
trembles indeed when a few pray together. Some members
of the body are given faith in large proportion which then
can serve as a shield for your protection. Some others have
the word of God in a special measure, and this can stand
as the sword of the Holy Spirit. When one or several of

them wield the sword—that is, when he or they use the word of God—this serves to help you. We must realize that spiritual warfare is preeminently a *joint* battle.

JANUARY 12th

Trust in Jehovah with all thy heart, and lean not upon thine own understanding. Proverbs 3.5.

How very hard it is to depend on God! How difficult it is for the wise to trust! How arduous for the talented to rely on the Divine! Oftentimes we become active without waiting on God for special strength. For us to deny our talent, to become utterly helpless before God and to not depend on talent but completely on the Lord, is most difficult. The Lord wants us to deny ourselves and our power and to acknowledge our weakness and helplessness in every word and deed. Except the supply of God comes forth, we cannot say a word or do a work. Only in such manner as this does He want us to depend on Him.

When a child is small, he leans on his parents for everything; but once he grows up he possesses such power and wisdom in himself that he seeks independence instead of dependence. Our God desires us to have a permanent relationship with Him as children so that we may continuously trust in Him.

JANUARY 13th

Keep thy heart with all diligence; for out of it are the issues of life. Proverbs 4.23.

Even though the spirit is the highest part of man, what really represents him is not his spirit but his heart. We may say that the heart is the real "I"; without question it is the most important thing in our daily living. Proverbs 4.23 means that all fruits which man bears outwardly come from the heart. Such is its significance.

The heart is the passage or channel through which life must operate. It is for this reason that God must first move upon our heart before His life can enter into us. If there be no sorrow of heart or repentance, God's life will not be able to come in. God has to touch our heart—causing us either to sense the pain of sin or to taste the sweetness of His love and the preciousness of Christ—in order to bring us to repentance.

JANUARY 14th

To whom God was pleased to make known what is the riches of the glory of this mystery among the Gentiles, which is Christ in you, the hope of glory. Colossians 1.27.

The truths of God are all organically related. There is a center towards which all truths are focused. What is the thread that is woven through all the truths of God? What is God's overall truth? Who is the Lord Jesus? We all might answer that He is our Savior. Yet very few can answer as Peter, who said that He is "the Christ of God" (Luke 9.20).

The center of God's truths is Christ. "The mystery of

God, even Christ," wrote Paul (Col. 2.2). A mystery is that which is hidden in God's heart. Never before had God told anyone why He created all things, including mankind. For a long time it remained a mystery. Later on, however, God revealed this mystery to Paul so that he might explain it. And this mystery, explained the apostle, is Christ.

JANUARY 15th

Wherefore if any man is in Christ, he is a new creature: the old things are passed away; behold, they are become new. 2 Corinthians 5.17.

Perhaps someone will argue that despite what the Scriptures say of his being a new creation, as he looks at himself he does not seem to be very new. I would again answer with this: How many sinners and saints are lacking in faith! Let me encourage us all to kneel and pray: "God, I praise and thank You, Your word says that if any man is in Christ he is a new creation. I am in Christ, therefore I am a new creation." Whenever the temptation comes to you which declares you are still the old man, if you will but answer with the word of God which says that you are in Christ and therefore you are a new creation, Satan will beat a hasty retreat. Or if you simply stand on the side of God's word and pay no attention to such temptation, you will also gain the victory. For victory does not rely on feeling but on the word of God.

JANUARY 16th

*The book of the generation of Jesus Christ, the son of
David, the son of Abraham.* Matthew 1.1.

Naturally the son of David is Solomon. To speak
of the Lord as the son of David intimates that the Lord is
to be as Solomon. In his lifetime Solomon did two things
in particular: he uttered words of wisdom and he built the
holy temple. But our Lord is greater than Solomon both as
a prophet and as a builder. He builds a spiritual temple by
sending forth the Holy Spirit.

Now in speaking of the Lord as the son of Abraham,
the Bible intimates here that He is to be like Isaac. In his
own day Isaac also performed two outstanding things,
which were his being offered on the altar and his marrying
Rebecca who was not a Hebrew. In like manner, our Lord
was offered as a sacrifice on the cross and by His death and
resurrection He has entered into a marriage union with His
church that is formed of the Gentiles as well as the Jews.

JANUARY 17th

*God, having of old time spoken unto the fathers in the
prophets by divers portions and in divers manners, hath
at the end of these days spoken unto us in his Son.*
Hebrews 1.1, 2.

The word of God informs us how in olden times
through His servants God revealed to mankind His heart
desire of love towards us by diverse portions and in diverse
manners, but man failed to comprehend. He thus had no
other way but to come himself to this world to become a

man, and this man is Him whom we know of as Jesus Christ.

The God of glory condescends himself to be a man. What humility is this! He who is far above all has emptied himself and taken upon himself the likeness of a man. Let me say that the entire earthly life of the Lord Jesus was for the purpose to express the loving heart of God towards men. In His thirty-three years on earth, Jesus manifested nothing less than the heart of God. The way He treated people on earth is the way God always treats us.

JANUARY 18th

For the word of the cross is to them that perish foolishness; but unto us who are saved it is the power of God. 1 Corinthians 1.18.

When we preach the cross, we should be those who can impart the life of the cross to other people. What pains me greatly is, that although many are now preaching the cross, the hearers do not seem to receive the life of God. People listen to our words; they appear to approve and gladly receive; yet the life of God is not present.

Man's thought, word, eloquence and argument can only stir up the human soul. They merely excite man's emotion, mind and will. Life, however, may reach man's *spirit*; and all the works of the Holy Spirit are done in our spirit—that is, in our inward man (see Rom 8.16; Eph. 3.16). As we in our spiritual experience let flow our life in the spirit, the Holy Spirit will send forth His life to the spirits of others and cause them to receive either regenerated life or the life more abundant.

JANUARY 19th

In the beginning God created the heavens and the earth.
Genesis 1.1.

People often laugh at the creation story myths circulated among the Chinese, the Babylonians, and other ancient peoples. No scientist bothers to refute these mythic accounts. And why? Because these traditions have no intrinsic value; therefore, they are not worth any special attention. People's attitude towards the Bible, however, is quite different. Their very effort to resist the Scriptures proves the power of the Bible. The fact that they do not treat this Book the same as they treat the traditions of the nations demonstrates the ascendant position the Bible holds.

Who can read the first chapter of Genesis without being impressed by its uniqueness? Rather common, yet so marvelous! The facts are presented in such a straightforward manner that there is not a trace of theorizing. There is no attempt to argue and to prove the authenticity of the facts presented. The Author is not bound by the book since He is so much bigger than that about which He writes. He far transcends the universe simply because He is God.

JANUARY 20th

Now therefore arise, go over this Jordan, thou, and all this people, unto the land which I do give to them . . . Every place that the sole of your foot shall tread upon, to you have I given it. Joshua 1.2, 3.

All who were now to enter Canaan were people of faith. They crossed the Jordan River by laying hold of

God's word. But after they crossed Jordan, did they immediately possess all the land? Satan will never make such a concession to God's people. The walls of Jericho were tall and the gates of the city were tightly shut. Had we been there in such a situation, we would probably have gone to God and complained, saying: "You said You had given us the land of Canaan. We have crossed the River, but now the walls of Jericho are so tall and the gates of the city are so securely shut. Has not Your word fallen short?" The children of Israel, however, did nothing of the sort. They believed in God's word and laid hold of His promise. They encircled the city once every day till on the seventh day they encircled it seven times; then they shouted, and in response the walls of Jericho collapsed. And thereafter they conquered one city after another.

JANUARY 21st

I John . . . was in the isle that is called Patmos, for the word of God and the testimony of Jesus. Revelation 1.9.

Due to his faithfulness to the word of God and to the testimony of Jesus, John was exiled to the island of Patmos. From the human viewpoint, John's staying in this isolated place was too lonely and pathetic an experience; yet he neither murmured nor complained, because he knew for whom he suffered. Praise and thank God, it is in just such an environment that the glorious Christ appeared to him and gave him new revelation and a renewed trust. Oh, for John at that time the earth was receding and heaven was opening. This reminds us, does it not, of Joseph in the tower, Moses in the wilderness, David in his constant tribulation, and Paul in bonds. How these all received fresh revelations! John, then, followed in the footsteps of these men and received a vision he had never known before. He came to know the Lord who sits on the throne.

JANUARY 22nd

But when he saw the wind, he was afraid; and beginning to sink, he cried out, saying, "Lord, save me." Matthew 14.30.

In walking upon the water, Peter should not have looked at the strong wind. He has the word of the Lord; he therefore ought not look at the wind and the waves. In looking at these things he easily forgets the Lord's word. Without the word, one should never walk on water in the first place, even if everything is calm. Since walking upon the water does not depend on the wind and the wave, one should never look at these matters. One should look only at the Lord.

JANUARY 23rd

Then said Jesus unto his disciples, If any man would come after me, let him deny himself, and take up his cross, and follow me. Matthew 16.24.

Denying self means disregarding one's self or renouncing one's privileges. To deny oneself denotes a setting aside of the self in seeking the mind of God, so that in all things he may not follow his own mind nor be self-centered. Only such kind of people can follow the Lord. This is of course self-evident, for how can anyone follow the Lord if he follows after himself?

"And take up his cross, and follow me"—This is even deeper than denying the self. For self-denying is only the disregarding of self whereas taking up the cross is obeying God. To take up the cross means to accept whatever God has decided for the person and to be willing to suffer according to the will of God. By denying self and taking up the cross we may truly follow the Lord.

JANUARY 24th

Strengthened with all power, according to the might of his glory, unto all patience and longsuffering with joy. Colossians 1.11.

As the power of God works within, peace and harmony are seen among believers. The might of His glory is the greatest of God's power. Having obtained such glorious might, we are able to perform a rather miraculous feat beyond any human expectation: "unto all patience and longsuffering with joy" is the greatest manifestation of the power of God. To be patient with a troublesome believer is more difficult than to pray and receive an answer from God. It is hard to be patient, but the power of God enables us to do so. We see that when a Christian receives the working and the filling of the power of God, he is able to be at peace with people as well as to be patient and forbearing.

JANUARY 25th

*I say the truth in Christ, I lie not, my conscience bearing
witness with me in the Holy Spirit.* Romans 9.1.

In regeneration our conscience is resurrected. The
blood of the Lord Jesus washes the conscience to make it
clean and sensitive. The Holy Spirit testifies in our conscience concerning our conduct. If we commit wrong, the
Holy Spirit will reprove us in our conscience. Let us observe
that whatever the conscience condemns has undoubtedly
been condemned by God. Consequently, if our conscience
declares a thing wrong, it must be wrong. It should be
repented of and confessed, and be cleansed by the precious
blood of the Lord. We can serve God without fear only
with a pure and clear conscience.

JANUARY 26th

*Why beholdest thou the mote that is in thy brother's eye,
but considerest not the beam that is in thine own eye?*
Matthew 7.3.

In the preceding verses (vv.1, 2), the Lord warns us
not to judge but instead exhorts us to be merciful. Here He
tells us how improper it is to judge. There is no question
about the beam in one's own eye, for if he sees the mote in
the other's eye it is certain that he has a beam in his own
eye. And why? Because to be able to see the mote, which
is so tiny, in your brother's eye proves that you must be an
expert in this respect. Because you have had experience in
such sin, you can most easily recognize it. As an old

Chinese adage goes: To catch a robber, use an ex-convict. Due to the multitude of one's own sins, a person tends to be more critical of his brother's fault.

JANUARY 27th

I have been crucified with Christ; and it is no longer I that live, but Christ liveth in me. Galatians 2.20.

There is one thing which we must pay special attention to, which is, that the full salvation which God has prepared for us must be received in full. I do not believe in sinless perfection—in the eradication of the root of sin; but I do believe God is able to save me to the uttermost. I do not believe the cross annihilates me, yet I do believe that there my Lord has died for me. Not that God has pulled out the root of my sin, but that He gives me a Christ to live in me. Formerly Christ died on the cross for me; now He lives in me and for me. The sphere of God's salvation is the sphere of my redemption. There is no need for us to retain ill-temper, uncleanness, anxiety, or fleshly lusts. God is able to deliver us from the bad but also gives us the good.

JANUARY 28th

So I was left alone, and saw this great vision, and there remained no strength in me; for my comeliness was turned in me into corruption, and I retained no strength. Daniel 10.8.

Abundance comes from enlightenment. As light shines upon us, we become rich. Yet strange to say, when we do receive such enlightening, we feel on our side as though decreased and not increased. For the shining of light will break up your past sight. It destroys what you originally had. Under the illumination of God, we actually do increase, and yet we do not feel it that way! If, all is as God gives light, you think you have increased, then in reality you have seen nothing. But in case you indeed see, so far as your feeling is concerned, you sense an emptiness as though you have never commenced walking on the spiritual pathway of life. One who is truly abundant senses himself to be nothing under the light of God.

JANUARY 29th

But your iniquities have separated between you and your God, and your sins have hid his face from you, so that he will not hear. Isaiah 59.2.

Once when R. A. Torrey was preaching at a certain place, a college student came up to him and said: "Formerly I believed in God, but lately I do not believe any more. I read this book and that book, until I eventually read God away." "Do not try to deceive me," Mr. Torrey responded, "for I too was a college student. I have read many books and I have a doctor's degree. But I have not read God away. Let me ask you a question. Now that you do not believe in God, how about your moral life?" To which the student replied somewhat candidly, "I must confess that my morality now is not as good as before." Whereupon Mr. Torrey concluded with a word well-spoken: "I need not argue with you. If you simply stop doing these bad things and begin to live more morally, God will immediately return." How factual that is, for many fail to believe in God not because they have good reasons to do so but simply because their multitude of sins hinders them from believing. They are compelled to be atheists.

JANUARY 30th

He that overcometh, I will make him a pillar in the temple of my God, and he shall go out thence no more: and I will write upon him the name of my God, and the name of the city of my God, the new Jerusalem. Revelation 3.12.

The Lord's vessel today is the same as that which was true at the beginning—which is to say, that it is not something individual but something collective in nature: in other words, the church.

People will perhaps ask concerning the overcomers in the church. True, the church is in great need of overcomers; but the testimony of these overcomers is for the benefit of the corporate entity, not for that of the personal. Overcomers are not a class of people who deem themselves to be superior, esteeming themselves as better than the others and pushing them aside. Not so. They instead work for the entire body. They do the work, and the whole church receives the benefit. Overcomers are not for themselves; rather, they stand on the ground of the church and bring it to maturity. Hence the victory of the overcomers becomes also the victory of the whole church.

JANUARY 31st

The servant therefore fell down and worshipped him, saying, Lord have patience with me, and I will pay thee all. And the lord of that servant, being moved with compassion, released him, and forgave him the debt. Matthew 18.26, 27.

The lord in the parable, but even more so our God in heaven, is moved with compassion not because the servant is willing to pay back, but because of the latter's repentance and humility and pleading for mercy. He knows very well that the servant is not able to repay, and so he forgives him the debt. "Released . . . forgave"—These verbs describe actions which happen in this age. If these actions can happen in the age to come, the Lord's righteousness will be compromised. Today God not only releases but also forgives all our debt. The grace of God always surpasses human expectation.

FEBRUARY 1st

What then is the law? It was added because of transgressions. Galatians 3.19.

We should know that God gives the law not for men to keep but rather for them to know that they cannot keep it. God already knows men have sinned, and yet people themselves do not know they have sinned. So God gives the law in order to cause men to know themselves and to know that they cannot keep the law. Surely our Lord knows all about this. It is absolutely inconceivable that the Son of God would come to this world to teach people to keep the law which is beyond their power to keep and which is itself added because of transgression. Since the law cannot keep people from sinning, would the Son of God come to tell them to do the impossible? God sends His Son to save men, therefore the Son will not insist on their keeping the law as a condition for their salvation.

FEBRUARY 2nd

Ye are not straitened in us, but ye are straitened in your own affections. 2 Corinthians 6.12.

The power of electricity is enormous, yet if a tiny switch is off, it can stop the current. The power of spiritual life is indeed great and spontaneous, but its growth will be limited if the conditions for growth are not met.

How, then, can this life be expanded? We should not forget that just as the acceptance of life commences from the heart so the growth of life must also start from the heart. Whether our spiritual life expands or not depends on how open our heart is towards God. If our heart is open to Him our life will expand; but if our heart is closed, it has no possibility of expansion. So, then, it comes back to the matter of the heart. We cannot afford to overlook this.

FEBRUARY 3rd

There was in a city a judge, who feared not God, and regarded not man: and there was a widow in that city; and she came oft unto him, saying, Avenge me of mine adversary. Luke 18.2, 3.

We who believe in the Lord Jesus stand on the Lord's side; accordingly, we cannot but reckon the Lord's enemy to be our enemy. Likewise, Satan the enemy of our Lord will not pass us lightly by and not oppose us. He considers the Lord Jesus to be his enemy, so that he is constrained to look upon the disciples of the Lord as his enemies also.

Such enmity deepens day by day. Since the enemy is so strong and we are so poor and desolate as is the widow, he uses all his powers to oppress us—causing us great loss. So much have we suffered at his hands that we cannot stress too strongly how Christians today are wronged by the devil. And if these wrongs are not avenged, we will suffer loss forever. What a pity that many of God's children are still unaware of the oppression of Satan.

FEBRUARY 4th

The kingdom of heaven is like unto a man that is a merchant seeking goodly pearls: and having found one pearl of great price, he went and sold all that he had, and bought it. Matthew 13.45, 46.

The pearl stands for the beauty of the church. The beauty of the church is the Lord's ornament. People will see this beauty and will praise the Lord.

The story of the making of a pearl is most interesting.

Pearls are produced by certain mollusks in the sea which are rather lowly-looking creatures. This betokens how the church comes from the most humble Christ. A smooth, lustrous, varicolored secretion, which is the very life of the mollusk, issues forth and surrounds a grain of sand or other foreign matter that finds its way into its shell. The mollusk must therefore be hurt if a pearl is ever to be formed. The roundness of the pearl depends on the tenderness of the mollusk. The more tender and sensitive the mollusk, the rounder the pearl. How sensitive and tender is our Christ.

FEBRUARY 5th

And apart from shedding of blood there is no remission.
Hebrews 9.22.

In the matter of forgiveness of sin, one may fancy that he has to try his best to do good in order to obtain forgiveness; but he has no idea as to how many years of good works he must do. Another imagines he needs to keep on praying until one day he thinks he has got peace. We must say, though, that these efforts are done in and of themselves.

We know we cannot compensate for sins by good works, for it is simply our duty to do good anyway. Neither can we petition God to forgive our sins. Nor can we pray till we forget our sins and thus regain peace. The only way to have them forgiven and cleansed is through the *blood*. "Apart from shedding of blood there is no remission." It is the blood of the Lord Jesus that solves the problem of our sins. It is His blood which cleanses us from all our iniquities (1 John 1.7). Do we believe?

FEBRUARY 6th

Even as he chose us in him before the foundation of the world, that we should be holy and without blemish before him in love. Ephesians 1.4.

Oh how great is this gracious calling! If you have never fallen or been weak, you may not appreciate the uniqueness of this calling. But in case you know somewhat of the depth of your weakness and uselessness, how dearly you will embrace it. You will say: "Thank God, You call me to be holy, You call me to be blameless, You call me to be perfect like You are." Praise the Lord, one day His purpose in choosing us shall be realized. No matter how weak and useless and blameworthy we currently are, one day we shall be brought by God to the place where we can stand before Him holy and without blemish as He is. This is what God has chosen us for and called us to. Since He has so desired, it shall certainly be done.

FEBRUARY 7th

For it is as when a man, going into another country, called his own servants, and delivered unto them his goods. Matthew 25.14.

This will be a test to the servants, because the servants may be faithful in the presence of the Lord, but true faithfulness will be seen only when the Lord is absent. The Lord delivers His goods to them for them to manage His property. The same is true with us today. The Lord has delivered His goods to us, and we are now serving the Lord whom we do not see.

Here in Matthew's account the Lord is recorded as not

instructing these servants what to do with His goods. He wants us to seek His will and do accordingly. Whoever knows the Lord's will and does it is fit to be rewarded. Not telling the servants what to do is a real test.

FEBRUARY 8th

Seeing that his divine power hath granted unto us all things that pertain unto life and godliness. 2 Peter 1.3.

Even though we cannot find the word "fact" in the Bible, we do discover many accomplished facts in the word of God. As regards God's promise there is the possibility of it going unrealized if we do not ask or do not fulfill the condition therein. But God's fact will not fail to be actualized in us for our lack of asking. Since it is already a fact, it needs no asking. Never once does God require us to do anything special in order to obtain His fact. We need only believe in it, and we shall have it. God's promise can be delayed, but God's fact is never detained. It is altogether impossible for us to accept God's fact and to wait for several years before He gives it to us. Whatever God has already accomplished and given us in Christ cannot be postponed to the future. For if God should hesitate in giving to us, it would be contradictory to fact.

FEBRUARY 9th

*With all prayer and supplication praying at all seasons
in the Spirit.* Ephesians 6.18.

For our prayer to be truly effective, we must spread out our prayer like a net. What does this mean? It means we must pray with all prayers so that nothing is left out which should be prayed for. We will not allow anything to slip away. Without such a "prayer net" we will not be able to obtain good results. A person who knows how to pray knows how to pour out his heart desire completely before God. He will use all kinds of prayers to surround as with a net the thing he prays for so that the adversary can do absolutely nothing. Nowadays our prayers are too loose, they are not tight enough. Though we may use many words, our prayers are not well-rounded, thus providing the enemy loopholes through which to make his attack. But if our prayers are like spreading nets, the enemy will have no opening by which to get in. And thus shall our petitions before God be realized.

FEBRUARY 10th

*Who then is greatest in the kingdom of heaven? And
[Jesus] called to him a little child, and set him in the
midst of them.* Matthew 18.1, 2.

The Lord concretely demonstrates His points as well as speaks forth in parables. By setting the little child in the midst of the disciples He is able tangibly to draw a comparison between the two parties. A single glance at the little child will tell the observer his height, weight, age, experience, and so forth. There is not even the need to inquire. A quick look will do.

If having been born again one can keep himself always humble as a little child, this man is the greatest in the kingdom of heaven. Unfortunately, many forsake this condition. Though they are but children, they act like grown-ups. To "become as little children" (v.3) is the one condition for entering the kingdom of heaven, and *to hold on to* this condition becomes the very basis for subsequent greatness.

FEBRUARY 11th

Now on the first day of the week cometh Mary Magdalene early, while it was yet dark, unto the tomb, and seeth the stone taken away from the tomb. John 20.1.

Many there are who only know the preciousness of the Lord's work and do not know the preciousness of the Lord himself. What makes Mary Magdalene different from other people is that she treasures the Savior himself, not just the salvation she receives. Many people there are from whom demons are cast out, but one alone seeks after the Lord—even Mary Magdalene. Though other women also came to find the Lord, the first one who arrived at the tomb was Mary Magdalene. She came early on the first day of the week, while it was yet dark. She cared for nothing but finding the Lord. Well has one brother said this, that after the Lord Jesus died, the whole world in Mary's eyes had become a vacuum! The whole world could not at all bewitch her heart, because one person alone had already captivated her. Her heart was fully possessed by the Lord.

FEBRUARY 12th

Blessed are they that hunger and thirst after righteousness: for they shall be filled. Matthew 5.6.

Once a Christian physician said to a preacher, "Spiritual beginning and spiritual growth come from hunger and thirst. Many people feel neither hungry nor thirsty. How can we help them to feel so?" The preacher replied, "You are a physician. You know that there is life in man. Unless he is dead he will more or less have the desire for food. How, then, can you increase his desire for food? You give him some medicine to stimulate him until his desire for food becomes normal. In the same way, the one who has some inward feeling must learn to obey such an impulse. If you obey this little feeling your hunger and thirst will increase a little. More obedience results in stronger hunger and thirst. As your inward feeling grows stronger, you obey a little more; and as you obey still further, your inward feeling increases that much more. More obedience means more inward feeling. Thus you immediately realize you are inwardly alive."

FEBRUARY 13th

We know that we have passed out of death into life, because we love the brethren. 1 John 3.14.

All who have passed out of death into life love one another. All who have become members of the same spiritual body love one another. Such love comes from life and it flows spontaneously. Could a person be considered a child of God if, after answering affirmatively that he is a Christian and after being reminded that as a Christian he ought to love other Christians, he then says, "I will start to love other Christians tomorrow if you say so"? Oh let us see that everyone who is truly born from above and has the life of God spontaneously loves all who are members together with him in the body of Christ. Whether he is reminded or not, he has a consciousness of loving the brethren.

FEBRUARY 14th

And I heard a great voice in heaven, saying, Now is come the salvation, and the power, and the kingdom of our God, and the authority of his Christ. Revelation 12.10.

Authority (Greek, *exousia*) is absolute, unrestricted freedom of action or right to act. It denotes that incomprehensible strength to which everything must bow. People today stress power but neglect authority. Man sinned because he tried to overturn the authority of God. Lucifer became Satan because he wished to overthrow God's authority. He not only does not himself submit to the authority of God but also instigates men to rise up against Him too. When Christ shall come, however, He will crush Satan with His authority. The sword which comes out of His mouth is the power of His authority. Christians today ought to learn to submit themselves under the authority of God.

FEBRUARY 15th

But God chose the foolish things of the world, that he might put to shame them that are wise. 1 Corinthians 1.27.

Oh how men look for wisdom and power, but God seeks out the foolish and the weak. 1 Corinthians speaks of the wisdom and power of Christ; it also declares that God chooses the foolish and the weak. The Greeks look for wisdom and the Jews seek for miracles which demonstrate power. But God sets aside man's wisdom and power. For where there is human wisdom, there is also fleshly power. Human wisdom and power can only be effective in human affairs. If they are used in God's work they will destroy it.

God will only use the might and power of the Holy Spirit to accomplish His work. And this might and power are manifested through the foolish and the weak.

FEBRUARY 16th

When [Moses] was well-nigh forty years old, it came into his heart to visit his brethren the children of Israel. Acts 7.23.

In the Scriptures is to be found one particularly precious fact—that God treasures especially a heart which inclines towards Him. The story of Moses beautifully illustrates to us how a man had a heart desire to save the children of Israel for God's sake. Although he was not used by the Lord until he was eighty years old, Moses' heart desire began at forty, not later at eighty. After forty long years had elapsed, God still had not forgotten the desire of this man's heart.

This was also true of Samuel. Hannah his mother prayed to the Lord saying: "If thou wilt indeed . . . give thy handmaid a man-child, then I will give him unto Jehovah all the days of his life" (1 Sam. 1.11). Because Samuel's mother had this desire of her heart towards God, Samuel was afterwards called and used by the Lord to accomplish His plan for that particular dispensation. Whenever the Lord sees a heart desire towards Him, He treasures it.

FEBRUARY 17th

For he must reign, till he hath put all his enemies under his feet. 1 Corinthians 15.25.

Today, our Lord Jesus holds the keys of death and of Hades. He will wait until He wipes out all traces of rebellion. He has brought His own blood into the holiest of all, having purified the heaven, and ever since acting as the *priest* of God. At His return, all things shall be restored to God's original design. Then shall He be God's *King*. He with His overcoming saints shall rule this world from heaven. He shall instruct the inhabitants of the earth concerning the will of God and the way of worshipping Him. And the conditions of the millennial kingdom shall be similar to that of the world before sin entered in. Having restored all things to their original design, Christ will have fulfilled the eternal purpose of God.

FEBRUARY 18th

He commanded the multitudes to sit down on the grass; and he took the five loaves, and the two fishes, and looking up to heaven, he blessed, and brake and gave the loaves to the disciples, and the disciples to the multitudes. Matthew 14.19.

If the loaves are not in the Lord's hands, He cannot bless. After blessing, there must be the breaking. How people love the blessing but abhor the breaking. How can the 5,000 men be filled if there is no breaking? And how can the Lord break the loaves if they are not given over to His hand? The Lord always takes our consecration for real, and so He starts to break us. Sometimes after consecration there will come extraordinary things, such as the losing of someone you love or the losing of wealth. This is an indication of breaking, for breaking will not occur until you are consecrated.

FEBRUARY 19th

For thus shall be richly supplied unto you the entrance into the eternal kingdom of our Lord and Savior Jesus Christ. 2 Peter 1.11.

Immediately after the Great War in Europe, a great celebration was held in London. The war had just been concluded, and the soldiers had returned home for a triumphant march. As the soldiers marched on, the sound waves of applause and praise flowed incessantly. Rank after rank had passed by until suddenly the air was explosive with the tremendous waves of even greater applause and praise. Many who watched were moved to tears. And at one point the nobility saluted and the king removed his crown. And why? Because immediately behind the marching ranks came carrier after carrier of soldiers who had lost their limbs or had been terribly wounded in body!

Those who have suffered on earth and have forsaken something for the sake of Christ, they shall receive much on that day just as had the wounded soldiers received much during that triumphal march; louder applause, higher praise, and greater glory.

FEBRUARY 20th

And now, behold, I go bound in the spirit unto Jerusalem, not knowing the things that shall befall me there. Acts 20.22.

As the human body has its senses, so the human spirit has its sensing too. We call this sensing of the spirit "intuition," for it comes directly from the spirit. For instance, we may be contemplating doing a certain thing. It appears quite reasonable, we like it, and we decide to go ahead. Yet somehow within us is a heavy, oppressive, unspeakable sensing which seems to oppose what our mind has thought, our emotion has embraced, and our will has decided. It seems to tell us that this thing should not be done. This is the *restraint of intuition*.

Or take another yet opposite example. A certain thing may be unreasonable, contrary to our delight, and very much against our will. But for some unknown reason there is within us a kind of constraint, urge or encouragement for us to do it. If we do, we will feel comfortable inside. This is the *constraint of intuition*.

And he would have passed by them. Mark 6.48.

In verse 48 something very special is mentioned. It states that as He was walking on the water, the Lord "would have passed by them"! Many people are surprised when they read this: it seems as if the Lord is not going to the disciples. But actually there is no problem here. For since the Lord orders His disciples to go to the other side—to Bethsaida—then to Bethsaida will He naturally go upon coming down from the mountain. The Lord will not go somewhere else to wait for them. He seeks them in the very way which He has commanded the disciples to travel. Now if they had turned aside, the Lord would not have met them nor turned aside to wait for them. How serious this is.

I sometimes wonder if the Lord were to order me to be in Shanghai but I were to go instead to Nanking, whether I would be raptured when the Lord comes? For rapture takes place in the way of the Lord's appointment. And will I not miss the rapture if I am not there? Each one of us is responsible for where he is.

And they, having heard the king, went their way; and lo, the star, which they saw in the east, went before them, till it came and stood over where the young child was. Matthew 2.9.

"The star, which they saw in the east"—This was the same star which they had seen at first. If we wish to be assured of God's guidance, there should be the appearing of the star the second time after its first emergence. This is a spiritual principle. The second showing of the star verifies the accuracy of its first appearance.

God said to Abram: "Unto the land that I will show thee" (Gen. 12.1). If after the first step was taken there was no confirmation with the second word from God, this first step might be our own error. The revelation that follows a revelation proves the correctness of the earlier step. The verifying of a revelation with another revelation is a divine principle continually to be remembered.

FEBRUARY 23rd

But Moses' hands were heavy . . . and Aaron and Hur stayed up his hands, the one on the one side, and the other on the other side; and his hands were steady until the going down of the sun. Exodus 17.12.

Each of us is but one member of the body of Christ, and consequently we cannot live without the protection of other brothers and sisters. Even Moses' hands needed the support of Aaron and Hur. If even Moses needed the support of other members, what about us?

The gates of Hades cannot prevail against the church. This very thing the Lord Jesus himself promised and declared (see Matt. 16.18). Yet our Lord has never promised God's children that they could be independent or leave the church. Spiritual warfare is not a personal affair, it is a body task. And hence, in order to obtain the needed protection, we must go to the brethren. Let us never think of ourselves as individually competent and "go it alone."

FEBRUARY 24th

Know ye not that they that run in a race run all, but one receiveth the prize? Even so run; that ye may attain. 1 Corinthians 9.24.

Soon after a person is saved he is set by God on a specific course that lies ahead of him. The entire life of a Christian can be likened to running a race. Yet this is not a racing towards the goal of eternal life. On the contrary, only the person who has eternal life is qualified to run. No, the result of this race is that some of the participants are to be crowned while others will not be.

What is meant by the crown? The crown represents the kingdom. It signifies reigning, having dominion and glory. And thus to obtain the crown means to gain the kingdom —that is to say, to reign with the Lord Jesus. For a Christian, having eternal life is already a settled matter, but having the kingdom depends on how that Christian runs.

FEBRUARY 25th

For I know that in me, that is, in my flesh, dwelleth no good thing: for to will is present with me, but to do that which is good is not. Romans. 7.18.

Romans 6 speaks of our co-death with Christ; Romans 7 speaks of the battle between the new and the old lives; and Romans 8 speaks of the victory in the Holy Spirit. Both verse 6 and verse 11 of Romans 6 tell us that the death of our "self" is a fact. Why, then, do many— believing in this truth—fail to experience the victory of Romans 8? It is because they have not failed enough.

God will let a believer fall until he willingly acknowledges, "I am sold under sin! There is no good in me!" Not till then will he know that except a power comes from outside, he is hopeless and helpless. But then will we cry out: "Wretched man that I am! Who shall deliver me?" When he really perceives how corrupt he is, he will then know and acknowledge that unless Christ rescues him he cannot overcome sin.

FEBRUARY 26th

Holding forth the word of life; that I may have whereof to glory in the day of Christ. Philippians 2.16.

We must hold forth the word of life. We must bring out the word of life and lift it up for people to see. The Bible never implies we can testify only with our life and not with the lips as well. We should open our mouth to testify among our relations, friends, and those with whom we are in contact. It is true that Jesus in the Gospel of Matthew says, "Ye are the light of the world" (5.14); but in the same Gospel He also declares: "Every one therefore who shall confess me before men, him will I also confess before my Father who is in heaven" (10.32). If you are able to believe and to do, then believe also that you can shine with your life and testify with your mouth in the midst of those among whom you live. In so doing, Paul says you are perfect.

FEBRUARY 27th

*And when they came to the threshing-floor of Nacon,
Uzzah put forth his hand to the ark of God, and took
hold of it; for the oxen stumbled. And the anger of
Jehovah was kindled against Uzzah; and God smote him
there for his error; and there he died by the ark of God.*
2 Samuel 6.6, 7.

Before David was made king, the ark had been
captured by the Philistines. At that time there had been no
Uzzah to safeguard it; nevertheless, it was well able to defend itself. For recall that whenever it was removed from
place to place, it never once faltered, although it did not
have the care of either Uzzah or any other Israelite: the
Philistines could not do anything to it.

Now, though, the ark was back among God's own people. Did it therefore need any man to hold it? Here must we
see the sin of Uzzah. The ark was well able to defend itself
among enemies; would it now require the care of man
among the Lord's own people? God, you will remember,
had always wanted the ark to be borne by the Levites, but
the people of Israel had now put it on an oxcart. Yet should
it fall, this would have to be its own business. Any stretching of the hand of man would only destroy God's testimony. Hence God would not allow Uzzah to go untouched.

FEBRUARY 28th

Christ, who is our life. Colossians 3.4.

Christ is victory! Christ is patience! What we need
is not patience or gentleness or love, only Christ. He must
have the preeminence in all things. Christ lives out patience,

gentleness and love through us. What do we deserve but death. We are not fit for anything but death. When God created Adam He gave the latter a command to keep. Yet God does not *re*-create us in the same fashion. He instead puts us in the place of death while He himself lives out His will in us. We should not only see that there is a Savior who died in our stead on Calvary, but even more so realize that this same One lives in us and for us now.

FEBRUARY 29th

In whom we have our redemption, the forgiveness of our sins. Colossians 1.14.

Suppose a Christian has sinned and he asks God to forgive him. Do you know when God forgives him? Some say pray until there is peace in the heart, for this is the evidence of forgiveness. Are there not many who have committed many sins and yet their hearts are quite at peace? Are there not also many whose sins have been forgiven but they still feel unpeaceful? How utterly undependable is man's feeling. In case a Christian has sinned, how long will you tell him he must pray before he can receive forgiveness? Let it be known that over nineteen hundred years ago Christ had already borne your sins away; that you have already died in the death of Christ, and hence you have already received forgiveness.

MARCH 1st

The Father loveth the Son, and hath given all things into his hand. John 3.35.

In eternity past God has predetermined to establish a house over which the second person in the Godhead, the Son, shall rule. He has given all things to the Son as His inheritance. All things are of the Son, through the Son, and to the Son. The Father plans, the Son inherits whatever the Father has planned, and the Holy Spirit accomplishes all that the Father has planned. The Father is the Planner, the Son is the Heir, and the Holy Spirit is the Executor. The love of the Father towards the Son commences in eternity past. He is the Beloved of the Father. Even in eternity the Father has loved the Son. When the Son comes to the world the Father still declares, "This is my beloved Son" (Matt. 3.17). The Father loves the Son and has given all things into His hands.

MARCH 2nd

Now when the Pharisee [Simon] that had bidden him saw it, he spake within himself, saying, This man, if he were a prophet, would have perceived who and what manner of woman this is that toucheth him, that she is a sinner. Luke 7.39.

This sinful woman had continually incurred the mockery and disdain of men, plunging her into self-shame. Yet here was Jesus who—so holy yet so approachable—permitted her to stand behind Him and weep at His feet. She wept as a means of pouring forth her agony due to sinning; she wept to discharge the hidden things in her heart;

she wept to complain that there was no deliverer; and she wept to express her hope of a Savior. However, her weeping did not gain Simon's sympathy; it instead precipitated his silent criticism. Indeed, the tears of sorrow for sin was something a self-righteous Simon could never understand. But this Jesus understood! He first corrected Simon and then testified for the weeping woman, saying, "Her sins which are many are forgiven." This forgiveness has become a gospel to many great sinners ever since.

MARCH 3rd

Pray ye therefore the Lord of the harvest, that he send forth laborers into his harvest. Matthew. 9.38.

Here is one of the greatest spiritual principles: Whatever the Lord has in His heart to do, He first calls the disciples to pray. Only after they have prayed to the Lord of the harvest to send forth laborers are they sent out by Jesus. The chain of prayer is (1) initiated by God, (2) prayed by men, and (3) the work accomplished in accordance with God's will. God answers prayer so as to achieve His will. And this is why one once said that prayer is laying down tracks for the will of God to run on.

Jesus asked the disciples to pray that the Lord of the harvest would send forth laborers. After a while, those who were sent out were these very disciples. As we pray for a certain thing, God is preparing us to be willing to do the very same thing.

MARCH 4th

*In those days cometh John the Baptist, preaching in the
wilderness of Judea.* Matthew 3.1.

The emphasis of John's work is different from that
of our Lord's work. John stresses repentance, because he is
sent to prepare the way of the Lord. For this reason he
stands in a different position from that of the Lord with
respect to the world.

John makes the wilderness his home, whereas the Lord
accepts the city as His inn. John comes to make people
weep, but the Lord comes to make them dance. John causes
people to weep, as though he were wearing sackcloth; the
Lord, however, causes people to dance, as though He were
supplying the music. A complete salvation is first to weep
and then to dance. In other words, repentance plus belief.

MARCH 5th

*And the eye cannot say to the hand, I have no need of
thee: or again the head to the feet, I have no need of you.*
1 Corinthians 12.21.

The Lord distributes His work to all, and everyone
has his share. We must not think of ourselves more highly
than we ought to think. We should be faithful to the portion which the Lord has given each of us; but we should
also respect the portion He gives to others. Many young
people possess a kind of competitive attitude in which they
are always comparing what they have with that which
others do not have and what they do not have with that
which others have. Actually, such comparison is absurd.
How can we add a chair to a table? Are they one or two?

A table plus a chair equals a table and a chair. If we are asked which is better, the hand or the eye, we can only answer that the hand and the eye are both good. He who has seen the body of Christ recognizes the functions of all the members. He looks at himself as only one among many members. He will not project himself to a distinctive position in order to compare himself favorably with others or even to occupy another's place.

MARCH 6th

Knowing this, that our old man was crucified with him, that the body of sin might be done away, that so we should no longer be in bondage to sin. Romans 6.6.

The sin here points to that sinful nature which reigns in man. The old man speaks of the self which delights in listening to sin. And the body of sin means this body of ours which is sin's puppet and which actually sins. Thus sin reigns within as master. It directs the old man to cause the body to sin. The old man represents all which comes from Adam; the old man naturally inclines toward sin. He it is who steers the body to sin. In order for us not to sin, some have suggested that the root of sin needs to be eradicated from within; whereas others have expressed the thought that we must harshly suppress the outside body. Yet God's way is totally different from man's. He neither eradicates the root of sin nor ill-treats the body; instead, He deals with the old man. "Our old man *was* crucified with him."

MARCH 7th

If any man would come after me, let him deny himself,
and take up his cross, and follow me. Mark 8.34.

We do not know what the way of the cross is. We
do not realize that all which comes our way is permitted by
God. Whatever is against our will, whatever causes us to be
misunderstood, makes us suffer, blocks our way, or shatters
our hope is a cross given by God to us. Yet how do we face
such a thing? Do we resist in heart? Do we complain to
people? Do we long to avoid these difficulties?

Whenever God allows a cross to fall on us, He has a
particular reason. Each cross has its spiritual mission, that
is to say, it is sent to accomplish something special in our
life. If we endure according to God's will—as the Lord
Jesus endured the cross (noting, however, that *His* cross is
to atone for sin whereas *ours* is not)—our natural life will
be further dealt with and we shall have a greater capacity
for being filled with the resurrection life of the Son.

MARCH 8th

But be ye doers of the word, and not hearers only,
deluding your own selves. James 1.22.

We often misunderstand the word "do." We take it
to mean that after we have heard and known the word of
God we must try our best to do what we have heard and
known. But this is not the meaning of "do" in the Bible.
True, we need to will to do what we have heard. Yet the "do"
of the Scriptures is not the doing with our own strength, it
is instead allowing the Holy Spirit to *live out* through us the
word of the Lord which we know. It is a kind of life, not

just a kind of works. And in having the life, we will quite naturally have the works. But to produce a few works cannot be deemed fulfilling the "do" of the Bible. We ought to exercise our will to cooperate in life with the Holy Spirit so that we may live out what we know.

MARCH 9th

For the foolish, when they took their lamps, took no oil with them: but the wise took oil in their vessels with their lamps. Matthew 25.3, 4.

The foolish prepared no oil apart from what was already in the lamp. The wise have extra oil in their vessels. Oil in the *lamp* speaks of the Holy Spirit who dwells in every regenerated person. A Christian, even a beginner, has the indwelling Holy Spirit.

But oil in the *vessel* means more than the indwelling of the Holy Spirit; it speaks of being *filled* with the Holy Spirit. The indwelling Holy Spirit is received at the time of regeneration, but the filling of the Holy Spirit comes through continual seeking following the moment of regeneration. Each believer has the Holy Spirit, yet not all have the fullness of the Holy Spirit. People may not be able to detect whether or not we have the oil twice over; and we may indeed get by without any trouble today, but on that future day we will be found out. Are we willing to pay the price?

MARCH 10th

No man rendeth a piece from a new garment and putteth
it upon an old garment; else he will rend the new, and
also the piece from the new will not agree with the old.
Luke 5.36.

The Bible does not tell us to improve ourselves,
since the Lord has already done it all. Jesus Christ has
borne our sins on the cross; and there He says, "It is finished." He has completed the work and nothing is therefore
left to be done. Today we do not need to do anything except
to confess that our garment is torn, that we are corrupted
and are unable to do any good, and to ask Him to give us
a new garment. But if you will to do good, you will have
to will it again and again and again. You ought to know
that aside from trusting the redemption which the Lord
Jesus has accomplished once and for all, there is no other
way of salvation.

MARCH 11th

And to wait for his Son from heaven, whom he raised
from the dead, even Jesus. 1 Thessalonians 1.10.

A brother during the first year of his salvation
spent much time in searching the Scriptures. He studied
especially concerning the second coming of the Lord. He
managed to analyze the events surrounding the Lord's
return. And as a result, he felt fairly proud of himself. One
day he met a sister who had deep experience with the Lord.
They conversed together on the second coming. She,
however, did not analyze as he did. What she stressed was
how to wait for the Lord's return. On that day, that brother

learned a deep lesson. He had been one who *talked* about the second coming of the Lord Jesus, but here was another person who was *waiting* for the Lord's return. Whoever merely talks about Jesus' second coming is poor, whereas the one who waits for the Lord's return is quite rich.

MARCH 12th

Looking unto Jesus the author and perfecter of our faith. Hebrews 12.2.

Our eyes must "look unto Jesus the author and perfecter of our faith." According to the original, it may be translated as "looking away unto Jesus"—meaning that we are to look away from all the other things around us and look only to Jesus. We do not look at anything but Jesus only. By looking to Him we may run the straight path. There are many things around us which may easily affect our attention and divert us from our goal. Only by looking away to Jesus will we be kept running in God's course.

MARCH 13th

Jesus therefore said, When ye have lifted up the Son of man, then shall ye know that I am. John 8.28.

We really ought to shout Hallelujah, for Christ "NOW IS"! Christians are in contact with this Christ who "NOW IS"—they are communicating with such a Christ as this—they are related to the God who NOW IS, so that all spiritual things are "now is" to the Christians.

How frequently you have burdens, trials, and problems. So you pray to God, yet no relief seems to come. The more you pray, the more complicated matters appear to be, as though no amount of prayers will help. You should realize that you have been standing on the wrong ground as you prayed, for you have been limiting God with time. You have been waiting for things to happen in the future, yet nothing has happened. Let us thank God that we can instead put the future and today together. Let us ask God to cause us to see that our Lord is the God who "NOW IS" — that whoever touches this point touches the secret of communicating with Him.

MARCH 14th

Ye know that the rulers of the Gentiles lord it over them, and their great ones exercise authority over them. Not so shall it be among you: but whosoever would become great among you shall be your minister. Matthew 20.25, 26.

The church is not like the nations which have their rulers and great ones. For 'all ye are brethren" (Matt. 23.8). It is not only unscriptural but also a violation of the command of the Lord to have a religious hierarchy. To rule and to teach people spiritually is permissible, but to rule over people positionally is absolutely forbidden. The bishops, elders, pastors, teachers, and so forth in the Bible are spiritually instituted. We should faithfully serve the Lord and seek to please Him only. It is sinful to entertain the thought of gaining a higher position through service.

MARCH 15th

For we must all be made manifest before the judgment-seat of Christ. 2 Corinthians 5.10.

From the time we believe in the Lord, whatever we do or do not do will all await a time of reckoning. Reckoning here has nothing to do with salvation. Our walk (see 1 Cor. 3.10–15), speech, and even thoughts will all be presented at the judgment seat. If our faults are under the blood, they have already been judged and will therefore not be recalled. But if they are not repented of and have not been put under the blood, there will have to be an accounting of them. Accordingly, let us learn to judge ourselves. The grace and love of God are manifested in the blood of the Lamb, but on the other hand His righteousness and holiness are revealed at the judgment seat of Christ. He will not overlook our unholiness.

MARCH 16th

This I say therefore, and testify in the Lord, that ye no longer walk as the Gentiles also walk, in the vanity of their mind. Ephesians 4.17.

The vanity of the mind is what we commonly call building castles in the air. It is a vain thought. The mind of such a person is fully occupied with a kind of vain thought. There was once a story about a man who was asked to pray at the conclusion of the preacher's sermon. As he did so he could not help praying about his fifty-two strings of money (at the time, coins in China were tied to strings). This man's mind was preoccupied with the vain thought of money. How, then, could the life of God be released? Through this example, we can see that a person, thing, or event may each become a kind of vain thought and occupy our mind. Whenever our mind is usurped by any vain thought, God's life is choked.

MARCH 17th

Worthy art thou, our Lord and our God, to receive the glory and the honor and the power: for thou didst create all things, and because of thy will they were, and were created. Revelation 4.11.

When God created man He gave him a free will. There thus exist in the universe three different wills; namely, the will of God, the will of Satan the enemy, and the will of man. People may wonder why the Lord does not destroy Satan in a moment's time. The Lord could, but He has not done so. And why? Because He wants man to cooperate with Him in dealing with Satan. Now God has His will, Satan has his, and man has his too. God seeks to have man's will joined with His. He will not destroy Satan all by himself. We do not know entirely why God has chosen this way, but we do know He delights in doing it this way—namely, that He will not act independently; He looks for the cooperation of man. And this is the responsibility of the church on earth.

MARCH 18th

And out of the ground made Jehovah God to grow every tree that is pleasant to the sight, and good for food; the tree of life also in the midst of the garden ... Genesis 2.9.

The tree of life signifies the life of God, the *un-*created life of God. Adam is a *created* being, and therefore he does not possess such uncreated life. Though at this point he is still without sin, he nevertheless is only natural since he has not received the holy life of God. The purpose of God is for Adam to choose the fruit of the tree of life with his own volition so that he might be related to God in divine life. And thus Adam would move from simply being created by God to his being born of Him as well. What God requires of Adam is simply for him to deny his created, natural life and be joined to Him in divine life, thus living daily by the life of God. Such is the meaning of the tree of life. The Lord wanted Adam to live by that life which was not his originally.

MARCH 19th

That, according as it is written, He that glorieth, let him glory in the Lord. 1 Corinthians 1.31.

Among the many truths which we have come to believe, there is none higher than that of our being "in Christ." This is the position the redeemed of the Lord obtain, according to the teaching of the New Testament. Nothing can be higher than this position, since the forgiveness of sins is in Christ, justification is in Christ, and sanctification is also in Christ. All spiritual blessings are in Christ. Everything is in Him. So that our being placed in Christ is a higher grace than any other we can ever receive. All that God gives to us is in His Son.

MARCH 20th

We love, because he first loved us. 1 John 4.19.

Love is not something forced. We love God because He first loved us. The more we love God, the closer we draw nigh to Him; the closer we are to Him, the better we know Him; and the better we know Him, the more we love Him and thirst after Him. A saint of God once said: "God gives us a heart which is so great that He alone can fill it." We may bemoan the smallness of our heart; nonetheless, all who have tasted of God will testify that the heart He has given us is a great heart indeed—a heart so big that anything less than Him can never fill it, for God alone can fill it! How much, then, does *our* heart yearn after God?

MARCH 21st

Ye therefore shall be perfect, as your heavenly Father is perfect. Matthew 5.48.

We truly know the standard laid down in the Bible for a Christian. We as followers of Christ must not follow our own will but be righteous as God is righteous and seek with singleness of heart His kingdom. But are we really such in actuality? How frequently we sin. How often our heart is unclean, our temper often flares up.

In other words we ought but we cannot. Yet at the same time we acknowledge that Christ has already attained perfection. And hence all this demonstrates the fact that *only God himself can live up to the living standard He has established*. Put another way, we may say that it takes the same life to live the comparable kind of living. For example, only a bird can live a bird's life or an animal an animal's life. So that it may accurately be stated that only God can live God's life. And since Christ is God, therefore Christ alone can live God's type of living.

MARCH 22nd

For the mind of the flesh is death; but the mind of the Spirit is life and peace. Romans 8.6.

Just as the life of a man cannot afford to be momentarily interrupted, even so, the power given by the Spirit must always be renewed and supplied. What the Spirit of God does at one time may not be the same thing He will do every time. Each contact with Him brings in fresh power. Our communication with the Holy Spirit is not once and for all.

When, for example, we hear of other people's spiritual experience, we naturally will try to imitate. We expect God to lead us in the same way and grant us the same result. How often we are disappointed in this respect. God has to allow us to be frequently disappointed so that we will seek him by *directly* depending on the Holy Spirit.

MARCH 23rd

The Pharisee stood and prayed thus with himself, God,
I thank thee, that I am not as the rest of men . . . or even
as this publican. Luke 18.11.

Not only does this Pharisee trust in his own righteousness, but the Lord Jesus further states that he also "exalteth himself" (v.14). All who exalt themselves will go to hell. I am a preacher of the gospel, and I must say that in all the years of such ministry I have never seen a proud man saved. If anyone desires to be saved, he must acknowledge himself as a helpless sinner. He cannot save himself, nor can he rely on himself. He should confess that hell is his deserved portion and prostrate himself at the foot of the cross of Christ—asking for grace, and trusting in Jesus of Nazareth who was crucified in shame for his sake. How humbling this must be! Yet without humility, who will do it? Nothing under heaven requires more humility than believing in the Lord Jesus as Savior.

MARCH 24th

And I, brethren, when I came unto you, came not with
excellency of speech or of wisdom, proclaiming to you
the testimony of God. 1 Corinthians 2.1.

Every one of us has natural talent—some with more, others with less. We tend at first to depend on our natural gifts to proclaim the cross which we have experienced. How eagerly we expect our audience to adopt the same view and share in the same experience. Yet somehow they are so cold and unreceptive, falling short of our anticipation. We do not realize that we are rather new in our experience of the cross, and that our natural good talents need also to die with Christ. Not until we discover that the work done by relying on natural ability can only please men for a time but does not impart to their spirit the *actual* work of the Holy Spirit, do we finally acknowledge how inadequate is our beautiful natural talent and how necessary it is that we seek for greater divine power.

MARCH 25th

And thou shalt put the staves into the rings on the sides of the ark, wherewith to bear the ark. Exodus 25.14.

At the four feet of the ark were four rings of gold, and the staves of acacia wood overlaid with gold were put into these rings to bear the ark. The staves remained in the rings of the ark; they were not to be taken from it. This meant that the ark might be carried out at any time. Hence the ark had a double use: On the one hand, it was the center of worship, having been placed in the holiest of all where God and men met. If anyone desired to worship God he had to go before the ark to worship, for without it no worship was possible. On the other hand, it served as the guide to God's people—it went ahead, with the people of Israel following suit. They could not go just anywhere they wished; they were required to follow the lead of the ark. Here we see symbolically how Christ leads us in the way that lies before us.

MARCH 26th

*But we have this treasure in earthen vessels, that the ex-
ceeding greatness of the power may be of God, and not
from ourselves.* 2 Corinthians 4.7.

Do not think that there is very little in the earthen
vessel, which metaphor Paul uses to refer to our physical
body. We learn from Paul's second letter to the Corinthian
believers that there is a tremendous treasure in our earthen
vessels. But do we actually believe it?

God's children ought to know what they have obtained
at the moment of new birth. It may have taken only a
minute to have received the Lord and been born again but
it will need thirty or forty years beyond that moment to
discover what each received in that one precious moment.
No child of God can fully know on earth the extent of what
God has given him at the moment of regeneration. Nevertheless, blessed are those who know somewhat more.

MARCH 27th

*Seeing it is God, that said, Light shall shine out of
darkness, who shined in our hearts, to give the light of
the knowledge of the glory of God in the face of Jesus
Christ.* 2 Corinthians 4.6.

The primary work of God's Spirit and God's word
is to send light into darkness. Sin has so darkened man's
mind that if he is left alone he will have no knowledge of
himself as to how dangerous his position is and that perdi-
tion awaits him in the future. From the spiritual standpoint,
he is completely in the dark for he does not even know he
needs a Savior. Neither his affection nor his reasoning will

give him any light. But now the light of God comes. It shines into his heart. It actually sheds its light on the ruinous scene and reveals the fallen state of the creature. Nothing is changed except the darkness has been dispelled. None of the things revealed under the light can satisfy God's heart. Just as God's light shone upon the formerly dark world, even so, the Christ of God now shines upon the darkened heart of a sinner.

MARCH 28th

And whether one member suffereth, all the members suffer with it; or one member is honored, all the members rejoice with it. 1 Corinthians 12.26.

Let us take the example of a person who may have had installed on his body an artificial leg. Now although it may appear to be almost the same as the other real leg, it nevertheless has no life in it. It therefore has no body consciousness; for when other members suffer, this artificial leg does not feel anything—when other members rejoice, the artifical limb senses no elation. All the other members have the same awareness because they all possess the one common life.

Life cannot be simulated, nor does it need to be. If there is life there is no need to pretend; if there is not life there is no possibility to pretend. A Christian who sees the body life will invariably have body consciousness with other members of the body of Christ.

MARCH 29th

I have been a Nazirite unto God from my mother's womb: if I be shaven, then my strength will go from me, and I shall become weak, and be like any other man. Judges 16.17.

Samson was a man who was full of power. The source of his power was in his hair. And as soon as his hair was shaved, Samson's power was lost. What was there about his hair to make him powerful? This hair of Samson's, we must remember, was the hair of a Nazirite. And a Nazirite in Bible times was one who was fully consecrated to God. And hence all real spiritual powers derived from the measure of one's consecration to the Lord. If our consecration is superficial, we shall be like a paralyzed person who has no power. But if our consecration to God is absolute, we will find the power. Therefore, no matter how and where we seek, we must be mindful continually that power is conditional upon man's consecration.

MARCH 30th

And he spake a parable unto them to the end that they ought always to pray, and not to faint. Luke 18.1.

We need to get rid of an improper concept which holds that our God is very reluctant to answer prayer. To pray with persistency simply means that, having clearly recognized God's need, you keep on praying. Why does the Lord not answer immediately? Why should the days of His silence be prolonged? Here are at least two reasons: (a) that God needs a full reaction from His people concerning the thing with which He is concerned and in which He is deeply interested; and (b) that sometimes such constant prayer is necessary due to a certain kind of need or environment — because of the strongholds which Satan builds, more intensified prayer is required to destroy them.

MARCH 31st

The fruit of the Spirit is love, joy, peace . . . Galatians 5.22.

In examining the fruits of the Holy Spirit — which express Christian witness — we shall readily see that they are none other than selfless acts. What is love? Love is loving others without thinking of self. What is joy? It is looking at God in spite of self. Patience is despising one's own hardship. Peace is disregarding one's loss. Gentleness is overlooking one's rights. Humility is forgetting one's merits. Temperance is the self under control. And faithfulness is self-restraint. As we examine every Christian virtue, we will discern that other than being delivered from self or being forgetful of self, a believer has no other virtue. The fruit of the Holy Spirit is determined by one principle alone: the losing of self totally.

APRIL 1st

Come unto me, all ye that labor and are heavy laden, and I will give you rest. Matthew 11.28.

The Israelites in the ancient time only expected to have their burden *lightened* by Pharaoh instead of expecting total rest from their burden. The condition of the

Israelites may represent the condition of the people today. As they had only hoped for their burden to be lightened but not lifted, so men today ask merely for a lighter burden and less worry. Let me declare that what the Lord Jesus Christ gives is not less labor but total rest. Do you know what rest is? It means a ceasing from work. You who are bound by sins and pressed with many burdens have no rest. Then know that the Lord Jesus came to give you rest. You need not do anything; He will simply give it to you.

APRIL 2nd

And God said, Let there be a firmament in the midst of the waters, and let it divide the waters from the waters.
Genesis 1.6.

Concerning the Six Days of work, God pronounced each day's work as good except the second day. Did God forget? Not at all, for what He says or does *not* say is equally full of meaning. The Scriptures are God-breathed, word for word. He did not pronounce the second day's work good because the firmament or air is somewhat related to Satan. Is not Satan "the prince of the powers of the air" (Eph. 2.2)? Seeing that this firmament would be the habitation of Satan and his evil spirits, God did not sum up this day's work as being good. The air thus becomes the headquarters for the kingdom of darkness. For this reason, while we are meeting or praying, we need to ask God to clear the air by means of the precious blood of our Lord so that we may not be oppressed by the enemy.

APRIL 3rd

And let the beauty of the Lord our God be upon us.
Psalm 90.17 mg.

One day a Christian went to talk with a servant of God. Being somewhat fearful of criticism, this Christian exerted his utmost strength to keep himself humble during the conversation. His attitude as well as his word were quite humble in tone. But while he was trying to be humble, those who sat nearby detected the strain of it. Now if a person is truly humble, he has no need to exercise so much effort.

Can you say he was not humble? Well, he appeared to be so, but in point of fact it was man-made humility, and such belongs to the soul. For if God had worked in this brother, he could have been humble quite naturally. He himself would not have felt he was being humble, and those around him could have instead seen the work of God in him.

APRIL 4th

And [Moses] looked this way and that way, and when he saw that there was no man, he smote the Egyptian, and hid him in the sand ... But Moses fled from the face of Pharaoh, and dwelt in the land of Midian. Exodus 2.12, 15.

What did all this mean? Moses knew only his wisdom and power; he had yet to recognize his foolishness and weakness. God wanted to show him that in relying on himself there were things which he could not do. He sincerely wished to help God in saving the children of

Israel, but God had no need of any human help. People who try to help Him with their fleshly wisdom and power will never receive His approval. Many are rejected by Him not because they lack in wisdom and power, but because they are *too* wise and powerful. Hence God cannot use them. He has to set them aside and let them cool down. He will wait until their natural fire is extinguished before He will use them.

APRIL 5th

And he said unto them, Why are ye fearful? have ye not yet faith? Mark 4.40.

The Lord Jesus on one occasion said to His disciples, "Let us go over unto the other side" of the Lake of Galilee; but suddenly there arose a great storm, with the waves beating into the boat so much that it was beginning to fill up. The disciples therefore awakened the sleeping Jesus and cried, "Teacher, carest thou not that we perish?" Whereupon He arose and rebuked the wind and the storm. And the wind ceased, and there was a great calm. But then the Lord rebuked the disciples by saying, "Have you not yet faith?" Do let us see that since the Lord had commanded that they all go to the other side, the disciples and Jesus *would* get to the other side. The wind might blow harder and the waves might rise higher; yet nothing could hinder them from reaching the other shore because the Lord had said otherwise. Accordingly, what is of utmost importance is to *believe God's word*. If God says so, then *that* is enough; and nothing else matters.

APRIL 6th

Hast thou eaten of the tree, whereof I commanded thee that thou shouldest not eat? Genesis 3.11.

Is it a sin to know good and evil? Is it not virtuous to seek to know good and evil? For God knows good and evil. Is it a sin to be like God? Is it not a commendable thing to seek to be like God? How is it, then, that this act of Adam's becomes the very root of all human sin and misery? For what reason? Although such action on the surface appears to be good, Adam acted without God's command or promise. And in trying to obtain this knowledge outside of God and according to his own self, Adam sinned. Do we see the significance here of that word "independence"? All *independent* actions are sins. Adam had not trusted in God; he had not set himself aside in order to obey God; he had acted independently of God; and in order to obtain this knowledge he had proclaimed independence against God. And that is why the Lord declared that this was sin.

APRIL 7th

When he seeth the blood upon the lintel, and on the two side-posts, Jehovah will pass over the door, and will not suffer the destroyer to come in unto your houses to smite you. Exodus 12.23.

What did God say regarding the blood thus applied by the Israelites? He declared: *"When I see the blood, I will pass over you"* (Ex. 12.13). How significant is this word! The "I" is God himself. Passover therefore means that God passes over when He sees the blood. It is *God* who sees the blood, not the people who put it on. We will never see the full value of the blood of our Passover Lamb because we are *inside* the door, whereas the Blood is applied to the *outside* of the door. So that the Blood is not seen by us, because it is not given to us to see. We must consequently use faith. Though we may not see it or feel it, we simply believe, for the Blood is for God to see. The essential matter for us is: has the Blood been applied? If it has been applied, there is no more need to be worried.

APRIL 8th

I came that they may have life, and may have it abundantly. John 10.10.

An abundant life is a matured life. We know the difference between growing and arriving at maturity. A child will grow annually; but after he comes of age, it is no longer a matter of growth, but is to him a matter of maturity. He who only experiences the period of growing does not have abundant life; it requires the time of maturing to achieve abundance. All who deem the beginning to be the whole will consider themselves fully possessing everything. How harmful, then, initial experiences can be to entering into deeper experiences. A shallow experience may hinder us from having a truly deep experience; having superficial knowledge may hamper us from having deeper knowledge.

APRIL 9th

Whom we proclaim, admonishing every man and teaching every man in all wisdom, that we may present every man perfect in Christ. Colossians 1.28.

How could Paul do such a work? Immediately he explains: "Whereunto I labor also, striving according to his working, which worketh in me mightily" (v. 29). The word "mightily" may also be translated "with explosive power." In other words, what God worked in Paul was explosive power, and hence that which worked out of Paul was likewise explosive power. The apostle labored not by his soulical strength but by this divine explosive power. This power exploded within him unceasingly, causing him to strive diligently to present every man perfect in Christ. It is this power of life which enables us to labor more abundantly and strive more diligently.

APRIL 10th

And without controversy great is the mystery of godliness: God was manifest in the flesh . . . 1 Timothy 3.16 AV.

A person who really knows God manifests Him. And this is none other than living a godly life. Godliness is a great mystery, but since God has been manifested in the flesh (1 Tim. 3.16), this mystery has now become a revealed one. Think of it! Jesus of Nazareth is God manifested in the flesh! This glorious God-and-Man has manifested the holy and glorious life of God. And today, this life is in us and shall be manifested through us.

Let it be clearly understood that godliness is not a kind of ascetic exercise; rather, it is a kind of life consciousness, being in line with the character of God's life. For this reason the apostle Paul lists godliness among the things which a man of God should pursue: "But thou, O man of God, . . . follow after righteousness, godliness, faith, love, patience, meekness" (1 Tim. 6.11). On the day we are born again, God's "divine power hath granted unto us all things that pertain unto life and godliness" (2 Peter 1.3).

APRIL 11th

But the father said to his servants, Bring forth quickly the best robe, and put it on him; and put a ring on his hand, and shoes on his feet. Luke 15.22.

This prodigal had prepared a speech for his father, but he was so touched by the father's love that he could not finish his speech with the words, "Make me as one of thy hired servants." By carefully reading the context we find that he was given no chance to say so by his father. The latter had heard enough. Without waiting for his son to finish his speech, he ordered his servants to bring out quickly the best robe to put on his son, the ring to be put on his hand, and shoes to be put on his feet.

Such salvation as this reveals how God will treat you and me: it is not how we think we will be treated by Him. If it were according to *our* thinking, we would at best be a hired servant forever. We think of ourselves as sinners, but God declares we are children. We think we will perish, but He seats us at the table. There is absolutely no danger of saying too much about the grace of God. We think we are not worthy to be called sons, but He does exceedingly above that which we could ever think of.

APRIL 12th

Fear not, Paul; thou must stand before Caesar: and lo,
God hath granted thee all them that sail with thee. Acts
27.24.

He who really has God's promise is usually restful
and calm in his demeanor, for to him that promise is as
good as realized. When Paul met with danger from the sea
on his journey to Rome, he could stand among his fellow
passengers and declare: "Sirs, be of good cheer: for I
believe God, that it shall be even so as it hath been spoken
unto me." Let us further observe that "when he had said
this, and had taken bread, he gave thanks to God in the
presence of all; and he brake it, and began to eat." Such was
Paul's attitude towards the promise of God. This created
such a deep impression on his fellow passengers that they
were "all of good cheer, and themselves also took food"
(v.36).

APRIL 13th

And he died for all, that they that live should no longer
live unto themselves, but unto him who for their sakes
died and rose again. 2 Corinthians 5.15.

Let it be clearly recognized that selfishness is no
less evident in prayer than it is in other areas! How strong
are our opinions, desires, plans and pursuits! Self-denial
must be practiced everywhere. It is just as essential in
prayers as it is in action. We ought to know that we redeemed ones should live for the Lord—He who both died

and now lives for us. We must live wholly for Him and seek nothing for ourselves.

We often think of prayer as an outlet for expressing what *we* need — as our cry to God for help. We do not see that prayer is the asking of God to fulfill *His* needs. We ought to understand that God's original thought is certainly not the letting of believers achieve their own aims through prayer, rather it is God accomplishing His purpose through the prayers of the believers.

APRIL 14th

Lie not one to another; seeing that ye have put off the old man with his doings. Colossians 3.9.

To say less than what is required is lying; to be pretentious is also lying. Try to be an honest person, and you will know how difficult it is. I had a friend who one day in Kuangtung Province encountered a bandit demanding money of him. Being a Christian, he thought he could not lie that he had no money. Yet if he said he *had* money, the bandit would take all and leave him nothing. He finally acknowledged the fact of his money and let the bandit take all he had in his pocket. In such an emergency, he could easily have lied to try to save himself; but if he were to be true to the Lord, he could not tell a lie.

APRIL 15th

And [the two angels] say unto her, Woman, why weepest thou? She saith unto them, Because they have taken away my Lord, and I know not where they have laid him.
John 20.13.

Mary had not thought of the Lord's resurrection. Four times as recorded in the Gospel according to Matthew, the Lord had told His disciples that after He died He would be raised from among the dead. Yet Mary knew nothing of it. So that on that day all her hope had been shattered; and then she only desired after the Lord's body. Yet in spite of her ignorance, the Lord revealed himself to her because of her singular desire for Him.

The Lord appeared to Mary so as to satisfy a heart that was hungering and thirsting after Him. Here was a heart wholly occupied with the Lord, and hence He sought her out. Let me say that it is not that detrimental if we are somewhat lacking in knowledge; but to have a heart that will stir up the Lord is most precious.

APRIL 16th

This is my blood of the covenant, which is poured out for many unto remission of sins. Matthew 26.28.

What is the relation between blood and covenant? We may say that blood is the foundation while covenant is the document. The blood lays the foundation of the covenant and the covenant reveals the document established in the blood. Without the blood no covenant can be inaugurated, nor will it be effective. God enumerates in the covenant all the inheritance He is giving us, and this covenant He seals with the blood of the Lord Jesus. It is on the ground of this New Covenant of the blood of the Lord Jesus that we come into our spiritual inheritance.

APRIL 17th

Now about that time Herod the king put forth his hands to afflict certain of the church. And he killed James the brother of John with his sword. Acts 12.1, 2.

Today many love to read the excellent letters of Paul, to hear of the great works of Peter, and to learn of the wonderful visions of John, but they altogether forget about his servant James. Yet how can we overlook the fact that all works of God are based on what James represents?

If there is not the suffering of James, the Lord will not be satisfied. For in His very coming into this world, our Lord Jesus stood in the place of the rejected. And if we therefore do not suffer with Him—and no matter what good works we may perform—we cannot satisfy His heart. Peter himself once declared, "Forasmuch then as Christ suffered in the flesh, arm ye yourselves also with the same mind" (1 Peter 4.1). Only by suffering can we overcome all things and complete the eternal purpose of God.

APRIL 18th

Peter answered him and said, Lord, if it be thou, bid me come unto thee upon the waters. Matthew 14.28.

Believers should imitate Peter in being special and in following the Lord first. "And [Jesus] said, Come" (v.

29). The Lord's word is a promise. Without the Lord's promise it would be a senseless adventure. Some people may accuse Peter of being fond of showing off; but the Lord, far from scolding him, encourages him to come. His promise shows His approval.

People may think it is safer in the boat. There is no need to walk upon the water to follow the Lord. Yet we should realize that the life of a believer is a life of faith. It is easy to have and exercise faith within the framework of a corporate situation, but to have faith individually is hard. As a matter of fact, faith is personal. Peter walks upon the water by faith. And this is commended by the Lord.

APRIL 19th

This gospel of the kingdom shall be preached in the whole world for a testimony unto all the nations; and then shall the end come. Matthew 24.14.

God is pleased to see that the end of this age is coming soon so that His kingdom may be ushered in. But the children of God have their duty to perform. They should work together with God to bring this age to its end. Prayer is one of the ways, but testimony is also required. Let us all stand up for the "majesty" of the Lord Jesus as never before. Let us testify to His "government" more than ever. If we want to continue the work of the apostles we must testify to what they testified. How greatly the church has forgotten the victory, the authority, and the throne of Christ. Whoever dares to testify that "Christ alone is King; Satan is not" is really preaching the gospel of the kingdom of the heavens.

APRIL 20th

Even as Moses is warned of God when he is about to make the tabernacle: for, See, saith he, that thou make all things according to the pattern that was showed thee in the mount. Hebrews 8.5.

God has His foreordained plan as to the work of the building of the church. Regardless of large or small matters, He has His own specific way. As Moses was not responsible for the design of the tabernacle but only responsible to build it according to the pattern of the mount, so the glory of a servant of Christ lies not in his ingenuity in doing God's work but rather in his careful execution of what he understands to be the will of God. To know the Lord's counsel and to execute accordingly is the glory of Christ's servant.

A sister who has served the Lord for many years once said, "Man has absolutely no liberty in God's work." When Moses built the tabernacle, he had no freedom in deciding whether a small nail should be made of silver or of gold. He made every item according to what the Lord had commanded.

APRIL 21st

He that believeth on me, as the scripture hath said, from within him shall flow rivers of living water. John 7.38.

We need to pay special attention to the word "flow" here. Such a term does not suggest the use of platform tactics, a certain tone of voice, some profound psychology, some eloquence, argument or learning. Although all these may at times be helpful, they themselves are neither the living water nor the mechanism by which the living water issues forth. To "flow" suggests something most natural; it requires no human effort but simply follows the grade.

The life and power of the Holy Spirit appears to flow naturally through our spirit. Otherwise, no matter how passionately we preach, our audience will listen passively. And even if sometimes they may seem to pay full attention and may seem to understand and be moved, nevertheless, what we say can only draw a praise from their mouths without giving them the life and power to do what they hear. May we be the channels of God's life today.

APRIL 22nd

When the king came in to behold the guests, he saw there a man who had not on a wedding-garment: and he saith unto him, Friend, how camest thou in hither not having a wedding-garment? And he was speechless.
Matthew 22.11, 12.

In Oriental countries, the wedding garments are not prepared by the guests but provided by the host. The wedding garment is Christ, our robe of righteousness. We need to be clothed with Christ (cf. Rom. 13.14, Gal. 3.27). God has provided the wedding garment for us, but the man in the parable thinks his own garment good enough (self-righteousness).

It really does not matter if one is poor, because the king has already made provision. If anyone considers himself unworthy, the king has the wedding garment ready for him. What there needs to be a concern for is any unwillingness to take off the old and put on the new.

APRIL 23rd

For this is the love of God, that we keep his command-
ments: and his commandments are not grievous. 1 John
5.3.

Once a few sisters told me that for them obedience
was most difficult. Other sisters, they said, seemed to be
able to obey easily, but for them to do so, it was like bearing
the sufferings of the entire world. Let me say here and now
that if you have never laid down your will and surrendered
to God with singlemindedness, if you have never cast aside
what you treasure most and denied what you like best, it is
futile for you to think of walking in the way of obedience.
Unless you have had such a definite experience, you will not
be able to walk in the way of obedience.

APRIL 24th

For hereunto were ye called: because Christ also suffered
for you, leaving you an example, that ye should follow
his steps. 1 Peter 2.21.

Shame is given to Jesus by men; yet this He
despises. A cross is given Him by God; but this He endures.
He is not perturbed by men's misunderstanding, ostracism,
accusation, desertion, or condemnation. Not because the
shame is not serious; in point of fact, the shame He suffers
exceeds that which any other man has ever passed through.
Neither is it because His holy nature is insensitive to the
shamefulness of being insulted; actually His feeling is
much keener than that of others. The cross which God has
given Him is not light. What He has gone through before
men and the evil spirits and the holy angels is not without

hardship. Yet our Lord endures the cross. He accepts it and endures it. And the final result? He reaches the end triumphantly: "and hath sat down at the right hand of the throne of God" (Heb. 12.2) awaiting the moment of His glorious appearing.

APRIL 25th

In the world ye have tribulation: but be of good cheer; I have overcome the world. John 16.33.

Are you thinking of victory? The victory of Christ alone is your triumph. Do you want to overcome the world? Again, it is Christ who has overcome the world. Or do you expect God to do something for you some day? Let me say once again, no, since God has already done everything for you in Christ. Hence victory is not a present-day affair, because Christ has *already* triumphed. May God grant us such a revelation that we may see *what we already have in Christ*. If we do not believe, we will receive nothing; but if we do believe, we have everything. In Christ are victory, justification, sanctification, forgiveness, and every other spiritual blessing. God can do no more for us. If we be in Christ, all which is Christ's is ours. It is not drawing out of Christ something to nourish us, but entering into Christ so as to allow what is already in Him to flow in us.

APRIL 26th

The very hairs of your head are all numbered. Matthew 10.30.

God notices the minutest detail, therefore He is the greatest. He who is most powerful is He who suffers long. There is nothing in our life too minute for God's care and concern. The number of your hairs registered in heaven is exactly the amount of hairs you have on your head. In this connection, the story is told of a widow who moved to a small upstairs apartment. She asked God for a carpet which would fit the room. Someone sent her a carpet having the exact dimension of the room, but also an iron pad and a fire fork. She commented afterwards that though she forgot to ask for these two other items, God had not forgotten. This is the meaning of God having our hairs numbered.

APRIL 27th

For the body is not one member, but many. 1 Corinthians 12.14.

As Christians, we should admire and seek for spiritual things, but we ought not have any emulative pretentions nor any trace of jealousy. Our attitude individually towards spiritual work should be: What I can do I hope others can also do; and what I cannot do I wish someone else can do; I would like to do more as well as I would expect other people to do more. How I need to realize that I can only be a single vessel in the work; I cannot monopolize it. I dare not consider the work and its result as altogether mine. If I insist that everything must be done by me, I have not apprehended the body. The moment I apprehend the body of Christ, immediately I realize that both my labor and that of others mean gain to the head as well as to the body. And let all glory be to the Lord and all blessings be to the church.

APRIL 28th

Then was Jesus led up of the Spirit into the wilderness to be tempted of the devil. Matthew 4.1.

From Adam to Christ is approximately 4,000 years. Within these 40 centuries no one was able to claim himself to be the Son of God. But today a voice comes out of heaven, saying, "This is my beloved Son." Satan is therefore stirred to wage war against Him. As a matter of fact, Satan never lets any child of God go easily; he always attacks him. Sin, the world, and environment seem to be all at odds with God's children. Yet Christ is our forerunner.

Since Jesus proves himself to be the Son of God by going through great temptations, can we who belong to Him be exceptions? The first and foremost matter in the work of Christ is to prove himself to be the Son of God. Consequently, the beginning of the church is a confessing of Christ as the Son of God. What Satan with all his power cannot shake is the Son of God. If we stand on this testimony, we too shall overcome.

APRIL 29th

*Jesus of Nazareth ... whom God raised up, having
loosed the pangs of death: because it was not possible
that he should be holden of it.* Acts 2.22, 24.

Every time we muse upon resurrection we feel its
preciousness. Resurrection is that which death has no
power to hold. Death cannot contain it.

Never has any man entered into death and come back
to life again. People have died throughout all the ages and
the generations of mankind. And all who have entered into
death have been held by death and have not returned. But
there is one man who came out of death. And this man is
the Lord Jesus Christ. "I am the resurrection," Jesus said,
"and the life" (John 11.25). He is life, therefore all who
believe in Him shall never die; He is resurrection, therefore
all who believe in Him, though they die, shall live.

APRIL 30th

*We reckon therefore that a man is justified by faith apart
from the works of the law.* Romans 3.28.

The concepts towards the law in today's church are
of two opposite kinds: (1) People are saved by grace and not
by keeping the law; but to attain sanctification we must
keep the law. (2) Again, people are saved by grace and not
by keeping the law; and hence we need not keep the law
after we are saved, though we do keep the commandment
of grace. The latter concept is correct. The gist of the Letter
to the Romans is that no sinner can be justified by the
works of the law; while the theme of the Letter to the Galatians is that no saved person can be sanctified by the works

of the law. These two letters have sufficiently proven that neither justification nor sanctification comes by the works of the law.

MAY 1st

Take my yoke upon you, and learn of me; for I am meek and lowly in heart: and ye shall find rest unto your souls.
Matthew 11.29.

The attitude our Lord continually maintained while on earth was one of meekness and lowliness. For us who are Christians to find that rest of which He spoke, we need to do two things: first, to "take my yoke upon you"; and second, to "learn of me." A yoke is a wooden rod placed upon the back of an ox to keep it from moving freely so that it may work diligently. In the land of Judea, the yoke was always shared by two oxen instead of being placed on only one ox. The yoke was put on the ox by its master; and hence the Lord our Master says to us to "take His yoke upon us." This yoke is apportioned to us by God and not by man nor by the devil. It is given by God, and it is chosen by us.

Whatever is appointed by God, and if taken by us, shall make us happy. If I am satisfied, I will have peace. I have nothing to be unhappy about because I have not escaped from the yoke of God appointed to me.

MAY 2nd

Keep back thy servant also from presumptuous sins; let them not have dominion over me. Psalm 19.13.

From this verse of David's psalm we are shown that there are two kinds of sin before God: one is the sin of rebellion, the other is that of presumption. Not doing what one is told to do constitutes the sin of rebellion. Now we all know the sinfulness of this kind of sin; and from this sin we wish to be delivered. But please take note that besides the sin of rebellion there is also that of presumption, which is, that we do what we are not ordered to do.

To be active outside of the Lord's will is to be presumptuous. Do we know that it is equally sinful for us to act without God's order? It is reckoned as sin before the Lord if we work for Him without His command and instead work according to our own idea, even though we may view what we do to be most excellent. The prayer of David is for Jehovah to keep him away from presumptuous sin.

MAY 3rd

And in the midst of the candlesticks one like unto a son of man ... And his head and his hair were white as white wool, white as snow. Revelation 1.13, 14.

When the Bible speaks of the failing and change of man it says his hairs become grey (see Hosea 7.9). In this respect, our Lord does not have a single grey hair. But on the other hand, Proverbs states that "the hoary head is a crown of glory" (Prov. 16.31). Hence white hair means both experience, glory, and length of years. It also denotes holiness, for in Isaiah, God is recorded as promising to wash away men's sins that they may become as white as snow and as wool (Is. 1.18). Whenever we recall that our sins are washed as white as the head and hair of our Lord are white, we must marvel at the greatness of the Lord's grace.

MAY 4th

With all prayer and supplication praying at all seasons in the Spirit, and watching thereunto in all perseverance and supplication for all the saints. Ephesians 6.18.

We know that each time we are watchful it is because there is some danger ahead. Without any danger or enemy lurking about we would have no need to be vigilant. We must therefore be watchful over the time of prayer and supplication. We must find time to pray. If we wait until we are at leisure to pray, we will never have the opportunity to do so. All who desire to do intercessory work or to make progress in prayer life must "make" the time by setting aside a period for prayer. Let us guard this period and hold fast to it. We must pray the prayer of protection for our prayer time. Pray that the period of prayer may not be lost.

MAY 5th

And Jehovah spake unto Moses, saying, If any one sin, and commit a trespass against Jehovah, and deal falsely with his neighbor in a matter of deposit. Leviticus 6.1, 2.

If people were to entrust us with fifty dollars, we would probably be faithful. But if we were to be entrusted with fifty pennies, we would perhaps not be so honest;

because the amount is small, we will not consider them important. Nonetheless, such conduct would be dealing falsely with people, and it would cause us to lose our communion with God. If we are asked to carry a letter, we may not actually open it and read the contents, yet we may wish to examine the outside of it. Now to glance at it unintentionally would not matter, but it would be wrong if we wished to probe the secrets of others. Such can hinder our living and having intimate fellowship with God. I am afraid many do not study the Bible well because of such sin not being dealt with. If we are unfaithful and do not deal with it, we may lose that freedom of communion with God which is so vital to maintain.

MAY 6th

Therefore let us also, seeing we are compassed about with so great a cloud of witnesses, lay aside every weight, and the sin which doth so easily beset us, and let us run with patience the race that is set before us. Hebrews 12.1.

In running, two matters are absolutely important: the one is to lay aside every weight, and the other is to put away sin. Sin hinders progress the most. It disqualifies people from running. Sin is the trespassing of the rules; and he who would trespass the rules is not allowed to run a race. He is ordered to the sidelines. A believer ought to put off and forsake the sin which he knows. Be it jealousy, pride, uncleanness of heart, lies in the mouth, hasty temper, or unrestrained lust—it will make him unfit for the race. A Christian must stand on Romans 6.6 and 6.11 and reckon himself as dead to sin. He must forsake sins and must not allow sin to reign over him. He must also yield his members as instruments of righteousness to God. Whatever offends the Lord must be honestly confessed, repented of, and forsaken so as to obtain God's forgiveness.

MAY 7th

And I was with you in weakness, and in fear, and in much trembling. 1 Corinthians 2.3.

The message Paul preaches is the cross of the Lord Jesus Christ. What he proclaims is not in vain since he is a living channel of divine life. With the gospel of the cross, he gives birth to many. Yet in preaching the word of the cross, what about himself? He says this: "I was with you in weakness, and in fear, and in much trembling." He *himself* is a crucified person! Let us see that it requires a crucified person to preach the word of the cross. Here Paul has absolutely no confidence in himself. His weakness, fear and much trembling—his looking upon himself as totally useless without any self-reliance—are the sure signs of his being a crucified one. "I have been crucified with Christ," Paul once declared (Gal. 2.20). He further said this: "I die daily" (1 Cor. 15.31). It takes a dying Paul to proclaim the crucifixion. Without the true dying of self, the life of Christ is not able to flow out.

MAY 8th

Bring the fatted calf, and kill it, and let us eat, and make merry: for this my son was dead, and is alive again; he was lost, and is found. Luke 15.23, 24.

Let me give you a new thought today, which is the *joy of God*. On the night I was saved, the more I thought about it the merrier I became and the more I sang. I did not mind if there were neither rhyme nor tune. And such is the joy of being saved. Nevertheless, this Scripture verse tells us that it was the father who was joyful. It is therefore the joy of God in His saving a soul that is being expressed here. We usually think when a sinner is saved, how glad *he* is, and how glad *we* are. We fail to realize how joyful God the Father also is when He saves a sinner. If we see this, we can begin to understand the Father's heart.

MAY 9th

And in him ye are made full, who is the head of all principality and power. Colossians 2.10.

Today many Christians are in a dilemma. They appear to be unable to die. Today they are bad, and tomorrow they will still be bad. No matter how much they try to be good, they try in vain. Oh, let me say that it is an erroneous gospel if it calls upon you *to do it yourself*.

All is done for us by Christ. This is His work. We ought to reckon what has been done in Him. What the Lord Jesus has accomplished is to cause us to be perfect in Him; and the Holy Spirit incorporates within us everything which is in Christ. He has not only died but has also been resurrected. When Christ died, we also died; when He was resurrected, we also were resurrected; and when He ascended, we also ascended. Our inheritance in Him is in fact far beyond our expectation.

MAY 10th

And seeing them distressed in rowing, for the wind was contrary unto them, about the fourth watch of the night [Jesus] cometh unto them, walking on the sea. Mark 6.48.

It is better to suffer than to drift. Far better is it to be distressed in rowing than to sail with the wind, far better is it to go the difficult way than to go the easy way and drift. Drifting consumes no energy. Stop rowing and the wind will send us back to where we first began. Just compromise a little, let go somewhat, and the wind will send us back. To love the world requires no effort: to follow the world demands no strength. But to stand and be faithful to the Lord is a sure invitation to an encounter with a contrary wind, and soon we shall feel distress in rowing.

It is quite easy to return to the old place, but quite demanding of us to go forward. Yet now is the time to be faithful. May we walk in God's appointed way.

MAY 11th

For the word of God is living, and active, and sharper than any two-edged sword, and piercing even to the dividing of soul and spirit. Hebrews 4.12.

What is soulish? Soulish is that which is done by oneself. And what is spiritual? It is that which is done by God. And these two are radically different. A person can do something without any need for waiting upon God and trusting in Him. Such action is fleshly and it is soulish. But if a person cannot speak before God speaks, cannot move except God moves first; if he must look to God, wait and depend on Him—then that person and that action is spiritual. Let us thus ask ourselves if all we do is in the Holy Spirit?

MAY 12th

Beloved, let us love one another: for love is of God; and every one that loveth is begotten of God, and knoweth God. 1 John 4.7.

Once a son was born to a brother in Christ. He was asked, "Now that you have become a father, do you love your son?" His answer was: "A week before I was to be a father, I kept thinking how I should love my son. But as soon as my son was born—the moment I saw him—my heart quite naturally went out to him and I simply loved him." We see here how human love springs from a consciousness inside, it is not taught from outside. Likewise, all the children of God who are bought with the blood of the

Lamb and receive God's life and are baptized into the body of Christ cannot help but be moved from within to love one another as members of the same body.

MAY 13th

For himself hath said, I will in no wise fail thee, neither will I in any wise forsake thee. Hebrews 13.5.

A child of God asked Him for a promise concerning her livelihood. One day she read these words: "Be ye free from the love of money; content with such things as ye have: for himself hath said, I will in no wise fail thee, neither will I in any wise forsake thee" (Heb. 13.5). She was both surprised and gladdened by this word. Such promise is conditional: one must first be free from the greed of gain and be content with what he already has, before he can experience the Lord's abiding support and supply. She said amen and amen to this promise. In her past twenty years she on the one hand maintained the principle that "if any will not work, neither let him eat" (2 Thess. 3.10) and on the other hand experienced the Lord's causing neither a handful of meal in the jar to waste nor a little oil in the cruse to fail (see 1 Kings 17.8–16). The Lord had not failed her nor forsaken her.

MAY 14th

For if, while we were enemies, we were reconciled to God through the death of his Son, much more, being reconciled, shall we be saved by his life. Romans 5.10.

The death and the resurrection of Christ give us new life. Just as He died for us, so He was also raised for us (Rom. 4.25). Even as we need His death, so we also need His resurrection. The absence of either one of these will reduce the gospel to vanity. Through the death of the Lord Jesus we are delivered from all which belongs to Adam — that is to say, to the natural. By His resurrection we can enter into all which belongs to Christ — that is to say, to the supernatural. His death delivers us from the position and experience of a sinner in order that we may no longer be sinners. His resurrection makes us righteous, obtaining the position and experience of the righteous. "Wherefore if any man is in Christ, he is a new creature: the old things are passed away; behold, they are become new" (2 Cor. 5.17).

MAY 15th

Wretched man that I am! who shall deliver me out of the body of this death? Romans 7.24.

We all know that no rescuer dares to rescue a person who has just fallen into the water. A wise rescuer will wait until the drowning person has struggled enough in the water on his own and begun to give up struggling.

In like manner God today allows His children to struggle and struggle till they realize how futile is their effort since they are merely getting themselves into a more perilous position. The Lord will wait until their strength is exhausted and they themselves judge that they are dying. At that moment, their thought runs something like this: If God does not deliver me, I cannot maintain my lot even for a minute; if God does not save me, I will certainly die! Not until that very moment will God stretch out his saving hand. Whenever a believer ceases to trust in himself, God will wholly save him at that moment.

MAY 16th

What is it then, brethren? When ye come together, each one hath a psalm, hath a teaching, hath a revelation, hath a tongue, hath an interpretation. 1 Corinthians 14.26.

So Paul instructed the Corinthian believers. Some people come to a church meeting as if they were tourists or spectators. Coming in such a manner will doubtless bring death to the meeting. Let this not be so. Let there be a mutual supplying of one another in all the meetings. Like the physical body, all the member parts of the spiritual body of Christ are incessantly communicating with each other: no part can stop where it is. If any part should cease communicating, it stops the flow of the life of God and brings in death to the body. No member can stop communicating or fellowshiping without doing damage to the church.

MAY 17th

And Jesus seeing their faith saith unto the sick of the palsy, Son, thy sins are forgiven. Mark 2.5.

Alas, how often sin damages man's body as well as causes pain to the heart. We readily acknowledge that many sicknesses are attributable to natural reasons, such as infection or over-exhaustion. But the Bible also reveals that some sicknesses are the consequences of sin (Mark 2.5, John 5.14). If a sickness is due to sin, whether hidden or manifested, the sinner certainly knows about it. What can he say and do except express regret and to mourn. In the case of the palsied man, the Lord knew the cause of this particular sickness. So that first He said to the man sick of the palsy, "Son, thy sins are forgiven," and then spoke once more to him and said: "Arise, take up thy bed, and go unto thy house" (v.11). What a tremendous gospel this is! Such forgiveness as this has forever afterwards become a great gospel to all who are sick through sin.

MAY 18th

Which he wrought in Christ, when he raised him from the dead, and made him to sit at his right hand in the heavenly places. Ephesians 1.20.

The meaning of the ascension of the Lord Jesus is that God has given Him a place higher than all the powers of Satan. His heavenly place is an overcoming position above Satan. The latter is now under His feet, with no further opportunity to attack Him; for He now is the Lord and Head over all things.

The Lord himself is now leading His own people to take

this heavenly position with Him so that they may shine for Him on the one hand and overcome the powers of darkness which attack them on the other hand. Just as the light of the sun overcomes darkness, so the heavenly position of Christ overcomes the powers of darkness. And just as the moon and stars dwell with the sun in heaven, so Christians abide with Christ in the heavenly places.

MAY 19th

Not in fleshly wisdom but in the grace of God, we behaved ourselves. 2 Corinthians 1.12.

The principle of Christian living is to rely on the will of God and not on one's cleverness, to depend on the grace of God and not on our own wisdom. This is a lesson we need to learn.

Suppose some action is put before you, but you do not know whether to do it this way or that, or not at all. You have no idea which is right. So you begin to deliberate on the effect of whichever action you may take. If you do it this way or that, what will people say? You therefore try to be clever. How? To say or to do that which will meet the least problem and avoid the most opposition. By following this policy it means you have forgotten that God's children do not live on earth by human cleverness. To be a Christian is really quite simple. You merely ask one thing: "God, what do You want me to do?"

MAY 20th

Even as the Son of man came not to be ministered unto,
but to minister, and to give his life a ransom for many.
Matthew 20.28.

A living Christ cannot save us, only the Christ who
has died can do so. The Lord cannot save us by His living
on earth; He is able to redeem us only by His being crucified. Bethlehem, Nazareth, and Galilee will condemn us;
only Calvary will give us eternal life. Do not be surprised
at hearing this. How many would say Jesus is our example?
That He is a great Teacher, a great Rabbi? Many will praise
the Lord Jesus for His beautiful character, His high morals,
His great power, and His noble personality. Yet may I
observe that the better the Lord Jesus looks, the worse you
and I appear to be.

Let us praise and thank God that His Son does not
come into the world to be our example for us to imitate until we are gradually and finally saved. No, no! He sent His
Son to this earth to *die* for us sinners, to accomplish salvation for us. God does not require anything from us, since
He has done all.

MAY 21st

And as for you, the anointing which ye received of him
abideth in you, and ye need not that any one teach you;
but as his anointing teacheth you concerning all things,
and is true, and is no lie, and even as it taught you, ye
abide in him. 1 John 2.27.

A servant of God once told this story. A brother
came to him and asked whether he could do a certain thing.

"Do you know in yourself?" he inquired. To which the brother immediately replied, "I know." Some days later this brother came back again to ask the servant of the Lord about another matter. The latter answered him in the same way as before: "Do you know inside yourself?" "Oh, I know, I know," he again replied. The brother came back a third time, and for the third time the servant of God asked him, "What does your inside tell you?" And immediately he once more replied that he knew. At that moment God's servant said in his heart (though he did not utter anything with his lips): "Why, my friend, do you forsake the near and seek the far? You have something in you that will teach you concerning all things, and is true, and is no lie." Let me say here and now that this something is the law of life. It teaches us what we should or should not do.

MAY 22nd

To this end was the Son of God manifested, that he might destroy the works of the devil. 1 John 3.8.

As soon as we discern a work of the devil, we can pray as follows: "O God, Your Son was manifested to destroy the works of the devil. How we thank You, for He has destroyed the devil's works on the cross. But the devil is now again working. Please destroy his work in us, destroy his manipulation over our work, destroy his devices in our environment, and destroy all his works." When we pray, we may pray according to the current situation in which we find ourselves. If we notice that Satan is working in us or family or work or school or nation, we can ask God to destroy his work in that particular area.

MAY 23rd

He that loveth father or mother more than me is not worthy of me; and he that loveth son or daughter more than me is not worthy of me. Matthew 10.37.

The Lord demands us to give Him all. It will not do if we give Him a little less. It is not relative but absolute love He requires of us. Loving the Lord to the extent of wounding ourselves will bring us to the place of rejoicing in our loving Him. If we love but do not rejoice in love, we have not loved to the extent of being wounded. But for those who do, their experience will be, that as they are bearing the cross, they shall commence to sing.

"Worthy" must first be considered from the Lord's side. Is the Lord worthy of your love? The whole problem revolves around whether the Lord is worthy; not how much we forsake the Lord, but how much He is worthy of our service. If we regard as an extraordinary act a prince proclaiming the gospel, we remain ignorant of the glory and majesty of our Lord. Our Lord is worthy!—worthy to be served by all the elites of this world.

MAY 24th

Arise, O Jehovah, into thy resting-place; thou, and the ark of thy strength. Psalm 132.8.

As long as the children of Israel maintained their proper relationship with the tabernacle or the temple they were victorious, and no nation could overcome them. Even though their enemies learned how to fight while they themselves were not familiar with fighting, the children of Israel overcame all their enemies nonetheless. But the moment they had problems with the tabernacle or the temple, they were taken into captivity. Nothing else—whether they had powerful kings or great wisdom in themselves—mattered at all; the only concern which mattered was whether or not they had offended the ark of the tabernacle or temple. If the Lord had the preeminence, then theirs was the victory. So, too, with us today. In minding the victory of Christ, we also have the victory. Except we give Christ the highest place we are not able to overcome. Unless Christ has the preeminence in our heart we cannot overcome.

MAY 25th

And I will be to them a God, and they shall be to me a people. Hebrews 8.10.

What is God after in the universe? In Genesis 2 we learn that after God had created man, He merely hinted that man should exercise his free will to choose God's life. This passage did not openly state what God desired to get in the universe. In another passage, Genesis 3, we learn that man fell into sin, but again, this passage does not uncover what the devil wished to steal away. Things remained veiled, until the day when God in proclaiming the Ten Commandments began to spell out His heart desire.

The first of the Ten Commandments is: "Thou shalt have no other gods before me." The second is: "Thou shalt not make unto thee a graven image, . . . thou shalt not bow down thyself unto them, nor serve them; for I Jehovah *thy God am a jealous God . . .*" The third commandment is: "Thou shalt not take the name of Jehovah thy God in vain . . ." And the fourth is: "Remember the sabbath day, to keep it holy" (Ex. 20.3-8). These four commandments reveal the heart desire of God. It is none else than that *God desires to be God*. God is God, and He wants to be God among men.

MAY 26th

And he that doth not take his cross and follow after me, is not worthy of me. Matthew 10.38.

A burden is not a cross. Burden is something inescapable; the cross, however, is subject to personal choice and can therefore be avoided. What the first cross in history was, so the countless smaller crosses will be which shall follow afterwards: just as the original cross was *chosen* by the Lord, so the crosses for today must also be *chosen* by us. Some people assume that they are bearing the cross whenever they fall into some hardship or encounter some distress. This is not true, however, for these kinds of things may quite naturally happen to any person even if that person is not a believer.

What then is a cross? It must be akin to what the Lord Jesus himself has said: "My Father, . . . thy will be done" (Matt. 26.42). The Lord asks His Father not to answer as He the Son wills, but as the Father wills. This is the cross. To take the cross is to *choose* the will which the Father has decided.

MAY 27th

But he answered and said, I was not sent but unto the
lost sheep of the house of Israel. Matthew 15.24.

Why does the Lord say this to her? To give this
woman a handle to hold on to. Though He is sent to the
house of Israel, it is nevertheless only to the lost sheep that
He is sent. "The lost sheep" has a much wider scope. Is not
this woman a lost sheep? May she not receive grace? If only
she will acknowledge that she is a lost sheep. The Lord
throws out to her a distant thought. His not answering her
at first (v.23) is not a rejection; rather, a silent permission.
Although He does not open His mouth at the beginning,
His heart is aching with love to show her grace. Unless the
woman stands on the ground of a sinner, He is unable to
answer her request. Let us see that the silent delay of God
is not outright rejection. His delay is not an indication of
any indifference, He is instead waiting for us to come
around.

MAY 28th

Which we have as an anchor of the soul, a hope both
sure and stedfast and entering into that which is within
the veil. Hebrews 6.19.

Suppose we are on a steamer which has a huge anchor. What is the use of the anchor if it stays on the
steamer? It is to be cast into the water so as to stabilize the
vessel. It is not to stay put on the steamer. Likewise is it
with faith. Faith never believes in what is in us; faith casts
itself upon the Lord Jesus. It is cast from us to Christ. Let
me tell you, should the steamer be loaded with even larger

anchors, it will not be steadied unless those anchors are thrown into the water. The more we look at ourselves, the more disappointed we become. But if we cast the anchor of faith onto the cross of the Lord Jesus we shall have peace.

MAY 29th

But present yourself unto God, as alive from the dead, and your members as instruments of righteousness unto God. Romans 6.13.

Suppose, for example, that God has touched a certain matter in a sister's life. She struggles with Him for a long time and will not submit to Him. Although she likes to pray with people, her prayer is of no avail because she has not yet consented to God's demand on her. When she tries to help others, she finds she cannot do so in spite of her great effort. But one day the love of Christ so constrains this sister that she yields with tears to God. And after having thus answered God's demand, she now goes out to help people and they are truly moved. This shows that spiritual power comes from consecration. In the measure of your consecration will be the measure of the power which God gives you.

MAY 30th

The church, which is his body, the fulness of him that filleth all in all. Ephesians 1.22,23.

We should look to God for grace that we may see what the body of Christ is. Our lives need the protection of the entire body; individual members are useless. The preservation of life is in my life not being destroyed as well as others' lives not being destroyed. If, negatively speaking, one blood vessel is broken and bleeds unceasingly, the whole body will eventually die. On the positive side, though, if the ear hears, the whole body hears; if the eye sees, the whole body sees. What one member receives, all the other members share in. Thus we must learn to live in the body; let us learn not to think of ourselves more highly than we ought to think, let us learn to treasure the church, and let us learn to walk with all the children of God.

MAY 31st

But his lord answered and said unto him, Thou wicked and slothful servant, . . . thou oughtest therefore to have put my money to the bankers, and at my coming I should have received back mine own with interest. Matthew 25.26, 27.

This servant's poor showing is attributed in the parable entirely to his laziness. D. L. Moody once said that it is hard for a lazy person to be saved. We can at least say that no lazy person will receive a reward. Let us not allow our gift to remain idle because it is small. Let us not wait for a more convenient or more promising time to serve.

"Thou oughtest therefore to have put my money to the bankers"—Gift may be distributed to others for trading. We should contact one or more people. However little our gift may be, it must not go unused. Why not at least *put it to use* to save one soul, help one life, or comfort one person?

JUNE 1st

And they called Rebekah, and said unto her, Wilt thou
go with this man? And she said, I will go. Genesis 24.58.

When Rebecca was asked if she would go with the
steward of Abraham, she answered: "I will go." She thus
left her father's house. After leaving her father's house,
Rebecca rode on a camel and journeyed through the
wilderness. This signifies the way of suffering (the camel
here signifies suffering). Only thus could she have helped
Isaac and pleased him. All Christians should tell the Lord:
"Henceforth I am willing to lay down everything, including
any person, event or thing, for Your sake." Otherwise, when
God says to us today to forsake a certain thing, we shall
reply that we cannot for it is too painful. Tomorrow if He
would challenge with another matter, we could again respond with: "No, I cannot because that is too painful." It
may appear that God is very hard on us. Why? Because we
have never left our father's house. "Forget also thine own
people, and thy father's house: so will the king desire thy
beauty" (Ps. 45.10, 11).

JUNE 2nd

If also a man contend in the games, he is not crowned,
except he have contended lawfully. 2 Timothy 2.5.

Who in an athletic game would dare to step out of
the line drawn in such a race? All must run within the
assigned lines. And such is the meaning of 2 Timothy 2
which states that "if . . . a man contend in the games, he
is not crowned, except he have contended lawfully" — that
is to say, according to the rules. How very pitiful that many

Christians run zealously, yet they do not run according to the course *God* has set. Our own zeal, labor and activity cannot substitute for God's rule and will. Running outside the will of God leads to loss. Since the Lord has set the course before us, we must run in it before we may expect to win the reward.

JUNE 3rd

How that our gospel came not unto you in word only, but also in power, and in the Holy Spirit, and in much assurance. 1 Thessalonians 1.5.

Let us not be satisfied with merely meaningful words. We must seek the power of God. How many times people talk about the truth of the Holy Spirit without their having even a little of His power. What a believer lacks is none other than more of the life of God.

It is most interesting to notice that if a person understands the truth of God with his mind, he must frequently be exercised to grasp this truth. But if he knows the truth in the power of the Holy Spirit and maintains it in the same power as well, he will not need to grasp the truth in time of need as though like a drowning person grasping hold of a rope; rather, he himself will be grasped and saved by the truth through the Holy Spirit. This distinction is most evident.

JUNE 4th

Now while the bridegroom tarried, they all slumbered and slept. Matthew 25.5.

The parable of the evil servant (Matthew 24) teaches believers to be ready to meet the Lord today, while the parable of the ten virgins instructs us to be prepared for any unexpected delay of the Lord's return. Should the Lord tarry for 56 more years, will you still be ready to meet Him? If you set your lamp to burn only till midnight, the Lord may tarry until after that hour. Do not despise the testing of the Lord. The usefulness of the oil in the vessel is revealed in the Lord's tarrying.

JUNE 5th

Unto me, who am less than the least of all saints, was this grace given, to preach unto the Gentiles the unsearchable riches of Christ. Ephesians 3.8.

There may come a day when on the one hand you sense jealousy and pride and lust within you and on the other hand you sense no love nor humility nor gentleness in you. You ask the Lord to deliver you. You ask Him once, twice, many times. Until one day you are given revelation concerning the riches of Christ, and you realize how foolish of you to have asked for deliverance. You are given to hear this word of God: "My grace is sufficient for thee" (2 Cor. 12.9). And thus there is no need to ask, for the Lord says, "I am holiness, I am gentleness, I am full of grace." Everything is in Him. As God shows you the riches in Christ, you pass through a crisis. Then you will experience more and more of the grace in Christ.

JUNE 6th

But we will not glory beyond our measure, but according to the measure of the province which God apportioned to us as a measure, to reach even unto you. 2 Corinthians 10.13.

Each servant of the Lord has a measure of the sphere of work which God has apportioned to him; each believer has a divinely-appointed course to finish. If each one will stand in his post, do his share of work, and finish his appointed course, what a glory shall be seen!

A huge pillar is certainly essential to a house, but a small nail is not any the less needed. How can the church be established if each one in the church aspires to be a great revivalist or a great evangelist or a great teacher? Ought we not walk in the course of the Lord's will? We should not aim at a great thing; we should stand instead in the place of God's choice. If He wants us to do a small work quietly, we are happy to do it. For God does not seek "great talent"; He uses whoever is usable. May we be willing to take our place under the divine appointment.

JUNE 7th

And my speech and my preaching were not in persuasive words of wisdom, but in demonstration of the Spirit and of power. 1 Corinthians 2.4.

The least amount of self-reliance will unquestionably take away our reliance on the Holy spirit. Only people who have been crucified know and are willing to know how to depend on the Spirit of God and His power. Paul, for instance, has himself been crucified with Christ;

hence, when he works, he exhibits fully the spirit of the cross without any self-dependence. Because he uses the way of the cross to proclaim the Savior of the cross, the Holy Spirit and His power support Paul's testimony. May we say with our brother Paul: "Our gospel came not unto you in word only, but also in power, and in the Holy Spirit" (1 Thess. 1.5). For though we may speak movingly, what is the use if the Holy Spirit is not working behind our words?

JUNE 8th

But watch ye at every season, making supplication, that ye may prevail to escape all these things that shall come to pass, and to stand before the Son of man. Luke 21.36.

The Lord distinctly promises that the church may escape the Great Tribulation and "stand before the Son of man"—This no doubt refers to rapture. Nevertheless, there is a condition involved. Not for all who are simply born again, but for those born-again ones who watch and pray. "That ye may prevail"—If you watch and pray, you may prevail. Hence the promise is given to those who do these things. Does everyone in the whole church watch and pray? Let us pay attention to this.

JUNE 9th

But seek ye first his kingdom, and his righteousness; and all these things shall be added unto you. Matthew 6.33.

Prayer will be answered if it aims at letting Christ have the first place in all things. Seek first the kingdom of

God and His righteousness, and God will add to us all our needs. May we transform the time of praying for *our* needs into a time of praying for God's affairs. God will then hear the prayer we have uttered—that is, prayer for the things of God; but He will also hear the prayer we have not uttered—that is, prayer for our own affairs. If we would ask first that the Lord might receive His, He would cause us to receive ours too. One of the sweet experiences in the life of a Christian is to have prayer continually answered.

JUNE 10th

How much more shall the blood of Christ, who through the eternal Spirit offered himself without blemish unto God, cleanse your conscience from dead works to serve the living God? Hebrews 9.14.

This verse tells us to what degree Christ can save our conscience. His blood is able to cleanse it from dead works. Let me ask you about your conscience. Is it under accusation? If yours is constantly under accusation, you have not fully possessed what Christ has accomplished for you. The Lord saves us; and His blood cleanses our conscience. It is so cleansed by His blood that there is no more condemnation. When we gather together we may sometimes pray, "O God, we thank You for we have our hearts sprinkled from an evil conscience"; yet afterwards we are frequently troubled. This that happens simply indicates that we have only had our conscience covered or that it is at times overlooked. But the blood of the Son of God is able to cleanse us. He is able to save us to the extent of having our conscience totally cleansed.

JUNE 11th

I have the keys of death and of Hades. Revelation 1.18.

In Revelation 6.8 it is said that Hades follows death. In Revelation 20.14 we see that both Hades and death end up in being cast into the Lake of Fire. In these two passages just cited it would seem that both Hades and death have taken up personality. This would appear to be confirmed by such Scripture passages as Hebrews 2.14 which says the devil has the power of death and Matthew 16.18 which mentions the gates (or powers) of Hades. Behind death and Hades there is a personal devil who holds the power. But our Lord has risen from the dead. Over Him death and Hades have no more power; quite the contrary, He holds the keys of both. Here we see that far from death and Hades holding power over our Lord, the Latter has in fact overcome them!

JUNE 12th

After this manner therefore pray ye: Our Father who art in heaven, hallowed be thy name. Matthew 6.9.

The prayer which the Lord taught His disciples as recorded in the New Testament is a great revelation. That prayer unveils the heart desire of God, which is, that *God wants to be God.* Only God himself can use His name in heaven, but on earth His name is used by some people in vain. God seems to hide himself as if He is non-existent. But one day our Lord instructed His disciples to pray, saying: "Our Father who art in heaven, hallowed be thy name." He instructs us to pray in this fashion so that we may declare that He is God—He alone—and none else is.

We should be like the psalmist of old, proclaiming: "Glory ye in his holy name" (105.3). We should also declare, "O Jehovah, our Lord, how excellent is thy name in all the earth" (Ps. 8.1).

JUNE 13th

Now ye are the body of Christ, and severally members thereof. 1 Corinthians 12.27.

A member of a physical body is different from a body cell. Lacking a cell does not matter much, but the lack of a member in a body is unthinkable. How pitiful that the conditions of many Christians are like those of cells in the human body instead of members. Such a person seems to have no specific use in the body of Christ, neither does he fulfill his part. In any given church meeting his presence does not appear to add anything to the body of Christ, and his absence does not give the appearance to the body that it is lacking in anything. Were he to perceive the body he could not help but see himself as a member. Were he to perceive the body, he would know that it will suffer loss if he does not supply life to it.

JUNE 14th

For the showing, I say, of his righteousness at this present season: that he might himself be just, and the justifier of him that hath faith in Jesus. Romans 3.26.

The more that people see sin through God's enlightenment, the more they are sorrowful for their sins, and the more they appreciate the grace of forgiveness. Yet there are people who always fear that God will not forgive because of the greatness of their sins, both in number and in gravity. Nay, they even go so far as to surmise that forgiveness will be too cheap should God really forgive them. All who embrace such wrong attitudes need to know the trustworthiness of forgiveness, for it is not without firm foundation.

Grace never reigns by itself, it reigns through righteousness (Rom. 5.21). Grace does not come directly to us, it comes to us indirectly through the cross. God does not forgive our sins because He pities us when He sees us repent, express regret, exhibit sorrow, and weep. No, God can never forgive on that basis. He must first judge our sins and then He forgives. A common notion held by many is that "grace and righteousness cannot both be preserved." Yet all who have been taught by grace will declare that in forgiving our sins God has kept both grace and righteousness intact.

JUNE 15th

Having the eyes of your heart enlightened, that ye may know what is the hope of his calling, what the riches of the glory of his inheritance in the saints, and what the exceeding greatness of his power to us-ward who believe. Ephesians 1.18, 19.

Sometimes men are tempted to say: "If only before the foundation of the world God had made such and such a decision, how good it would be." But Paul tells us that what God has predetermined before the foundation of the world is perfect and complete. Men may even be tempted to say: "Ah, if only today God would do such and such."

Yet God wants us to understand that everything has already been done on the cross and in resurrection.

Hence, Paul is not found praying that God may do a little more for us, neither that He will make His grace towards us a little richer, nor that He will manifest His power in us a little more. What Paul longs for us is not that we may obtain more of God but that we may see how glorious and rich and great is that which we have already obtained.

JUNE 16th

The disciples say unto him, Whence should we have so many loaves in a desert place as to fill so great a multitude? Matthew 15.33.

Those who say such words look only at the environment. The prime lesson of faith is to be rid of the "whence" in our thinking. No prayer of faith ever says "whence"; if God says so, that is enough.

The loaves given to the disciples for distribution represent resurrection. The loaves in the hands of the disciples originally can never multiply, but after being broken by the Lord, that which remains of the multiplied loaves after the feeding of four thousand men, besides the women and children present, fill up seven baskets. A life that has been dealt with by the cross is no longer natural but is supernatural and overabundant in supplying the needs of others.

JUNE 17th

Even so, I say unto you, there is joy in the presence of the angels of God over one sinner that repenteth. Luke 15.10.

Have we ever thought of how each return and each obedience gives joy to the Father's heart? The peak of the gospel lies not in what the sinner receives but what God receives. How we should give ourselves wholly to Him. How much can we give to God? Let us not assume it does not matter if we grow a little bit cold. We should know what loss our little bit of coldness gives to God. Let us not rationalize that it is only a small thing to love the world and be mixed up with it. We ought to realize that this has much to do with our relationship to God: how this will cause much loss to the Father.

Consecration is not forced on us to put us down; rather, it enables us to enter the joy of God, that he may rejoice because of us. How wonderful this is! May we enter into the Father's joy today, and give God cause to be glad!

JUNE 18th

For sin shall not have dominion over you: for ye are not under law, but under grace. Romans 6.14.

In America there was once a Christian who had been able to overcome many things in his life except for four or five sins which he committed repeatedly. He confessed that his history was a story of continual confession. One day he read Romans 6.14. He accordingly prayed as follows: "Your word says sin shall not have dominion over me, but my situation attests that sin *has had* dominion over me. Nevertheless, today I believe in Your word, therefore I declare I have already overcome my sin." Later on, when one of the same temptations came his way, he would still fall if he looked at himself; but whenever he trusted in the word of God, telling God that His word could not be untrue, he experienced victory. And thus he lived a victorious life. Here is the most important thing for us to lay hold of: God's word. If you look at yourself, you shall be as corrupted as you were before. If you look at your environment, it will be as difficult as it has always been. But if you believe in God's word, you are able to overcome.

JUNE 19th

For from within, out of the heart of men, evil thoughts proceed ... All these evil things proceed from within, and defile the man. Mark 7.21, 23.

The heart which Mark speaks of is our natural heart. What is the condition of that heart? "All these evil things proceed from within," says the Lord. Oh, how much wickedness comes out of the heart! But in Matthew's Gospel we find the Lord declaring: "Blessed are the pure in heart" (5.8) — He is able to save the heart and change it from wickedness to pureness.

The way to have our heart saved is not by suppressing the evils within so that they will not come out; rather, it is by a cleansing from the inside out. If we attempt to cover or to seal up, let it be said that such is not salvation; because we have not yet been saved to the point of pureness of heart. We should inquire before the Lord as to how much evil thoughts, craftiness, and pride we have in our hearts.

If these be only suppressed within us, we merely cover them over and our hearts are still not saved. Does not God in fact say, "Blessed are the *pure in heart*"?

JUNE 20th

But I say unto you, Love your enemies, and pray for them that persecute you. Matthew 5.44.

The aforesaid actions are taken because there is love. If we are fretful, we will not be able to pray for our persecutors. The love in view here is neither due to liking nor to familiarity, rather it is because of mercy. We should never shut up a heart of mercy.

By acting according to verse 44 we may be sons of the heavenly Father, since we have exhibited His nature. Verse 45 ("That ye may be sons of your Father who is in heaven: for he maketh his sun to rise on the evil and the good . . .") shows us how liberal is the way God treats mankind. Were He like us, none would ever be saved. Only God can forget man's evil. Man does not possess the ability to forget evil; he does not have absolute forgetfulness.

JUNE 21st

That which we have seen and heard declare we unto you also, that ye also may have fellowship with us: yea, and our fellowship is with the Father, and with his Son Jesus Christ. 1 John 1.3.

Please note that the Gospels precede the Epistles. The Gospels first relate what Christ has done, and only then do the later Epistles *explain* what actually has transpired. First the experience of Christ, then the doctrine of Christ. First the life of Christ, then the teaching of Christ.

Martin Luther went through much suffering and hardship, yet he did not obtain justification. Not until one day God showed him that justification is by faith. Only by faith was he finally justified; and thereafter he presented the teaching of justification by faith. First the life, then the applicable doctrine. Let us not spend too much time in examining, analyzing, and researching a doctrine. All these are like reeds which will not support you when encountering real life difficulties. It is God who carries you through. First experience, then the doctrine.

JUNE 22nd

But Noah found favor in the eyes of Jehovah. Genesis 6.8.

During the days of Noah mankind sinned so terribly that their iniquity could be spoken of as being full; consequently, God destroyed them with a flood. Yet He was mindful not only of Noah and his family but also of many living creatures. He wanted to preserve their lives. So He made a covenant with Noah, saying: "I will establish my covenant with thee; and thou shalt come into the ark, thou, and thy sons, and thy wife, and thy sons' wives with thee. And of every living thing of all flesh, two of every sort shalt thou bring into the ark . . . And take thou unto thee of all food that is eaten, and gather it to thee; and it shall be for food for thee, and for them" (Gen. 6.18–21). In order to preserve their lives God even thought of their food. And thus this covenant reveals how loving and sensitive is God's heart towards man.

JUNE 23rd

For through him we both have our access in one Spirit unto the Father. Ephesians 2.18.

Trust means having the ability to entrust to, boldness to rely on, the full assurance to depend upon, and so forth. It really includes a very great deal. A spirit of trust is most essential to prayer and to the total Christian life. If our relationship with the Lord continually fluctuates — with our having neither assurance nor confidence — our entire life will be fatally wounded.

True trust is based on one factor, which is Christ himself. We have absolute privilege to draw near to God because Christ himself is that privilege which we have. This is God's provision. In Christ's name we may come to the Father at any time anywhere. We never approach the Father in our name or our condition because this is simply impossible. We come to see the Father in the name of the Son alone.

JUNE 24th

He that doth not take his cross and follow after me, is not worthy of me. Matthew 10.38.

To love the Lord is His only demand. Without denying self, no one can love the Lord. Here He does not mention His own cross. The emphasis here is taking up the cross. To be *laid on* the cross occurs only once: there He carries us. To *take up* the cross is a daily affair: here we carry Him.

What is meant by taking up the cross? It is submitting to God from the heart. In the Garden of Gethsemane our

Lord had his mind set on doing the Father's will. And so He went from there to take up the cross. Taking up the cross, therefore, is being determined to do God's will and nothing else.

JUNE 25th

Now when Pharaoh heard this thing, he sought to slay Moses. But Moses fled from the face of Pharaoh, and dwelt in the land of Midian. Exodus 2.15.

When God sets you aside, you may not understand His will. Again and again He places you there, without giving you favorable environment, so that you may submit yourself under His mighty hand. This is to test whether or not you will do His will, for your own will must be dealt with. This is a crisis you must face. The rejection of Moses by the children of Israel was of God. The seeking for his life by Pharaoh was also of God. His flight to the lonely wilderness was likewise of God. After having had numerous communications with God in the wilderness for forty years, he was finally taught by God, he at last realizing his total uselessness. He then no longer dreamed of saving the Israelites with his own ability. He no more thought of himself as a great and mighty man. He ceased to consider himself as being par excellence in the spiritual realm. He at last knew what he could not do. And that was precisely the place which God had wanted him to arrive at all along.

JUNE 26th

Seeing that ye have put off the old man with his doings, and have put on the new man, that is being renewed unto knowledge after the image of him that created him. Colossians 3.9, 10. *That ye put away, as concerning your former manner of life, the old man, ... and that ye be renewed in the spirit of your mind.* Ephesians 4.22, 23.

These passages underscore the fact that we should experience the perfectness of "the new man" in accordance with the life of God. "Put off," "put away" and "put on" are actions of the will. Believers need to exercise their will to reject all the works of the old man and to choose all the freshness of the new man. The apex of Christian living is the life of the will. With the will set, they shall be renewed in mind and knowledge according to the image of God. The mind is the battleground in spiritual warfare. It is *the* stronghold of the Adamic life as well as being that part of our life which is most corrupted by sin. If the mind be renewed, the image of God can easily be restored.

JUNE 27th

Thou shalt remember all the way which Jehovah thy God hath led thee these forty years in the wilderness, that he might humble thee, to prove thee, to know what was in thy heart. Deuteronomy 8.2.

Let us understand that God has no need for our defeats and failures—only we do. For while we experience smooth sailing, being often victorious and full of joy, we may regard ourselves as being fairly good and having possession of something that other people do not have.

Though we may not dare to boast openly of anything, nevertheless, when we make some progress in spiritual life or have some success in spiritual work we cannot help but conceive the thought that now we are truly holy and powerful and excelling quite well. In such a state as this, it is easy to become careless and to lose the attitude of depending on God. Accordingly, the Lord permits us to fall from glory to dust. We learn we are no different from the world's greatest and worst sinners. With the result that we dare not be self-reliant anymore but will in all things cast ourselves upon God with fear and trembling.

JUNE 28th

For hereunto were ye called: because Christ also suffered for you, leaving you an example, that ye should follow his steps. 1 Peter 2.21.

A sister once ruled her house like a queen, then got saved, and became almost like a maid. When she asked her parents for some pocket money and she was not given it as quickly as before, she was willing to lay aside her position and privilege as a daughter. Being now a Christian, you cannot expect your parents to necessarily treat you any more as their child or expect your friends to necessarily deal with you kindly as before. If they refuse to give you your rights, you should put yourself in God's hand and learn concerning the Lord, one "who, existing in the form of God, . . . [nevertheless] emptied himself" (Phil. 2.6,7). He never spoke for himself, therefore we should not speak for ourselves either.

JUNE 29th

The sum of thy word is truth; and every one of thy righteous ordinances endureth forever. Psalm 119.160.

After the translation of a certain Assyrian tablet, people enthusiastically reported that the Old Testament history was now being verified by that tablet. This is really turning things upside down. Does the word of God need any verification? Let us clearly understand that if the record on the Assyrian tablet coincides with that of the Bible, it only shows that the tablet has no historical error. And if they do not agree, it merely proves that the tablet is erroneous. In a similar way, if the teaching of science agrees with the Bible, the latter verifies the truth of science. But in case they do not agree, the Scriptures attest to the falsehood of science's hypothesis.

JUNE 30th

When he came down from the mount ... Moses knew not that the skin of his face shone by reason of his speaking with him. Exodus 34.29.

The lady who powders herself needs to look at the mirror frequently, but Moses' face shone often without his even being conscious of it. Whoever manifests the effects of God's working in him, that can be called spiritual. But the one who attempts to manufacture something must employ much strength; therefore he feels weary at being a Christian, although a Christian should never exericse his own strength in any case. We often judge that so long as a thing looks good it is probably all right, but God looks at the source as to whether it is of Him or an imitating in the power of the flesh.

JULY 1st

For this is acceptable, if for conscience toward God a man endureth griefs, suffering wrongfully. 1 Peter 2.19.

The rest of a Christian lies not only in his not owing anything to anybody but also in enduring whatever he is owed. Many young Christians had defrauded others before they were saved. But afterwards they try to be fair with people. When Christians now experience any unfairness they feel angry. They do not know that believers must not only be fair to others but must also endure any unfairness meted out to them by others. What the Lord received from others was certainly not fairness. In all frankness and fairness, He had no need to come to this world to become a man in order to save us. But for our sakes He was willing to endure all unfair treatment.

JULY 2nd

Whereunto I was appointed a preacher, and an apostle, and a teacher. 2 Timothy 1.11.

God always uses His *chosen* ones to do His work; He does not need volunteers for His task. Whoever is chosen by Him has absolutely no liberty. If any of His chosen ones desires the freedom to walk his own way, he will experience nothing but failure and pain. Yet if anyone is at all chosen, he will not be able to flee from God's appointed course. Even if he should flee to Tarshish (as did the prophet Jonah), he will be thrown into the sea and brought back by a great fish. There is no escape for such a one. A servant of God must never do anything according to his own will or conception, because the man whom the Lord selects is one who will only do the work which God has apportioned to him and run the course which God has prepared.

JULY 3rd

And the witness is this, that God gave unto us eternal life, and this life is in his Son. 1 John 5.11.

The testimony of John is confined to the Holiest of All—it is full of spiritual reality. He never touches on outward things but is always speaking on that which is *inward*, that is to say, the depths. Hence the word "life" is seen a great deal in both his Gospel, his letters, and the book of Revelation. The characteristic of his ministry is that of recovery after there has been a general falling away or spiritual declension. For at the time he wrote his letters, his Gospel, and Revelation, apostasy had become quite prevailing.

In view of this state of affairs, John stepped forward and spoke on the inner reality of things: which is life. John's testimony is therefore concerned with the last days. He leads people to the innermost recess to discover what a God they really have.

JULY 4th

Wherefore let us keep the feast, not with old leaven, neither with the leaven of malice and wickedness, but with the unleavened bread of sincerity and truth. 1 Corinthians 5.8.

What does leavened signify? It signifies malice and wickedness. *Un*leavened, on the other hand, means sincerity and truth.

The story has been told that once at passover time a carpenter in Judah searched carefully everything and everywhere to make his house as clean as possible in preparation for keeping the feast. But in the evening of the first day of the feast, he suddenly discovered that there was moldy bread in a bag. Not daring to touch it with his hand, he used two pieces of wood to pick the moldy bread out and then he burned it in the fire. How piously he kept this feast! This should impel us to ask ourselves how much time we Christians have spent in dealing with sins.

JULY 5th

They that wait for Jehovah shall renew their strength; they shall mount up with wings as eagles; they shall run, and not be weary; they shall be weak, and not faint. Isaiah 40.31.

I heard a missionary once say: if we are not able *not* to work for God, we will not be used by Him to save sinners; but if we are able not to work for God's sake, we will be used by Him to save people. This does not mean He is going to save souls without the instrumentality of the preaching of the gospel by men. Nevertheless, if a work is not of God's will, we must be willing not to do it. We must not act presumptuously. Without the command of God, we would rather be quiet than move ahead. And such kind of people will be sent by Him to save souls.

To do anything without being sent or ordered is like building a house on the sand or else like gold plating. It may stand temporarily or it may glitter for a while, but it will be destroyed at the judgment seat of Christ. Only those works that closely follow the command of God are useful.

JULY 6th

Jesus . . . who for the joy that was set before him endured the cross, despising shame, and hath sat down at the right hand of the throne of God. Hebrews 12.2.

The Lord Jesus looked at the joy that was set before Him and ran straight towards it. What is the joy? Did not He himself say, "Well done, good and faithful servant: . . . enter thou into the joy of thy lord" (Matt. 25.21)? This points to the joy in the millennium. True, our Lord obeyed God His Father according to His inherent nature. But in the Bible we find another fact, which is, that God's reward and promise—especially that of the kingdom—definitely had some influence on Jesus' life. Because of the joy that was set before Him, our Lord Jesus in His earthly race pressed onward bearing both shame and the cross.

JULY 7th

So then death worketh in us, but life in you. 2 Corinthians 4.12.

A death that can work must be a "working death"
— the life of death, even the life of the cross. For the sake
of the Lord Jesus, Paul is ready always to be delivered to
death. Notwithstanding unpleasant words, high-handed attitudes, cruel persecution, or unjustified misunderstanding,
he is quite willing to bear them all for the Lord's sake. Paul
will not open his mouth when he is delivered to death. Like
his Lord who could ask the Father to send twelve legions
of angels to help Him, he will under no such circumstances
adopt man's way to avoid these unpleasantries. He would
rather have the "living death" of Jesus — the life and spirit
of the cross — worked in him so as to show forth the spirit
of the cross in all his dealings. He reckons the cross as all
powerful, because it enables him to be willing for the sake
of the Lord Jesus to be delivered to death and to suffer
persecutions and hardships of the world.

JULY 8th

*And now why tarriest thou? arise, and be baptized, and
wash away thy sins, calling on his name.* Acts 22.16.

The Bible not only denies that baptism is merely a
ritual, it also reveals to us that baptism is a testimony. Why
do people go into the water? That they may testify before
God and men and angels and Satan that they have believed
in Jesus and that what Christ has accomplished is true,
perfect and trustworthy.

Ananias called Saul to rise up and be baptized. Why?

For the sake of washing away his sins. Yet Ananias did not suggest that baptism could get rid of sins, for it is not water baptism itself that washes away sins, but it is the reality which baptism expresses and testifies to that washes away sins. The water of the whole earth cannot wash away one single sin, yet what the water of baptism represents and testifies to—even the blood of the Lord Jesus—*is* able to wash away *all* sins. Have you believed? If you have, arise and be baptized to wash away your sins.

JULY 9th

The friendship of Jehovah is with them that fear him;
and he will show them his covenant. Psalm 25.14.

What kind of person may receive God's direction? They who fear God; because "the secret of Jehovah is with them that fear him, that he may make known his covenant to them" (same verse, Darby's translation). What is the meaning of "fear God"? To fear Him is to hallow His name—that is, to exalt Him. They who seek God's will with singleness of heart and obey Him absolutely are those who fear Him. To such as these will He tell His secret and show His covenant.

JULY 10th

For ye died, and your life is hid with Christ in God. Colossians 3.3.

Saints who have come into ascension life have the insight of the throne. They shall not be moved by anything.

All who are truly crucified with Christ are truly raised with Christ; and all who are truly raised with Christ are truly ascended with Christ.

By being in this ascended position the saints can enjoy more intimate fellowship with the Lord. And as a result, will not the awful condition of this world's dark night be made more manifest and the power of darkness appear to be closer by? Will we not possess further insight and will not Christ become greater? What a position this is!

JULY 11th

And the sword of the Spirit, which is the word of God.
Ephesians 6.17.

There are many believers who regard themselves as knowing a great deal. They think they can be more than conquerors by knowing many truths. Yet they are defeated again and again in their lives. Though they try with every effort to grasp these truths, they still find themselves helpless. For in the time of battle, the truths they know so well turn out to be like weapons of straw. They weep and shed many tears. Can the truths of God be wrong, or is there something else wrong? Oh, God wants them to see that the Holy Spirit alone can wield the Sword of the Spirit (which is the word and truth of God). For the flesh to use the Sword of the Spirit is like David trying to wear Saul's armor that was totally unfit for battling Goliath. Although they may well know the truth in their head, these people have not depended on the Holy Spirit to make such their life.

JULY 12th

From whom all the body fitly framed and knit together through that which every joint supplieth. Ephesians 4.16.

Because we are members of the body of Christ and members each in its part, we must seek how to help the body in gaining life and strength. In any gathering, even if we do not open our mouths, we may pray silently. Even though we may not speak, we can still look to God. If we have seen the body, we cannot say we are a person of no consequence. We will rather say: I am a member of the body, and hence I have a duty to perform. I have a word which I should speak, I have a prayer which I should utter. When I come to the meeting I must do whatever God wants me to do. I cannot afford to be a spectator. As we all function, the life of the entire gathering will swallow up all death.

JULY 13th

And [the Comforter], when he is come, will convict the world in respect of sin, and of righteousness, and of judgment. John 16.8.

No one who is truly awakened spiritually is unconscious of his sins. Like the prodigal son of Luke 15, he becomes aware, at the moment when he comes to himself, that he has sinned against his father as well as heaven. A person who is enlightened by the Holy Spirit will not fail to reprove himself for his sins (John 16.8). This is the time when he needs God's forgiveness. If he does not see his sin, he will not seek forgiveness. But once he notices it, he will spontaneously think of his guilt before God, the penalty of sin, the ceaseless suffering of hell, and the hope of salvation. Then and there is the gospel preached to us, proclaiming that the Lord Jesus has died on the cross and His blood has been poured out for the remission of sins. By His blood our sins are washed away. Upon hearing and believing the gospel we shall receive the remission of sins and the cleansing of our conscience.

JULY 14th

My son, give me thy heart. Proverbs 23.26.

Surrender is not a promising God to do His will, nor is it *making covenant* with God to do what cannot be done. To surrender is for me *to take my hands off my own life*.

Suppose you give a book to someone, yet your hand will not let loose of the book; will your friend be able to receive it? When we come to God we must say to Him, "I hand over to You all my good and bad, my likes and dislikes, my willing and not willing, my do's and do not's." Are we willing to do this? If we are not, there is nothing God can do for us. It is our responsibility to hand over our defeated selves. God is ever ready, waiting for you and me to do this one thing, to be willing to hand over these selves of ours.

JULY 15th

When ye pray, ye shall not be as the hypocrites: for they love to stand and pray in the synagogues and in the corners of the streets, that they may be seen of men. . . . They have received their reward. Matthew 6.5.

There are two different kinds of reward: that which comes from man, and that which comes from God. No one can have both rewards. If we wish to receive man's reward now we will not be able to obtain God's reward in the future. We cannot seek to enjoy great fame on earth and then have high position in the kingdom to come. If today's zeal and alms are for the purpose of getting fame and praise, there will be nothing to gain in the future before God. For this reason we should refuse today's reward.

What, after all, can the praise of man add to us? If we have our eyes opened we will seek only the glory before God and the angels; the rest will not count at all.

JULY 16th

Jesus therefore, being wearied with his journey, sat thus by the well. . . . Then cometh a woman of Samaria to draw water: Jesus saith unto her, Give me to drink. John 4.6, 7.

This asking for water is an expression of intimacy. Usually you are afraid of God, but you will not be afraid of one who asks you for water. You are fearful of God, but you will not be fearful of the God who asks you for water. You are frightened because you think of God as high and distant and terrible. But if you know that this lonely, weary and perspiring One (even as you are lonely, weary and perspiring) is God, you will believe in Him. How approachable and friendly is our Lord Jesus towards men.

JULY 17th

He that loveth father or mother more than me is not worthy of me; and he that loveth son or daughter more than me is not worthy of me. Matthew 10.37.

Once there was a brother who upon seeing the meaning of baptism in the Scriptures wished to be immersed. But his father did not approve of it. The son therefore experienced a great struggle in his heart at the time. His dilemma was that if he were immersed ne would hurt his father's heart; but if he were not immersed he would be disloyal to the Lord's word. As he was struggling in his heart over the issue, he was given a word by the Lord: "He that loveth father or mother more than me is not worthy of me" (Matt. 10.37). Here he encountered this matter of cost. Would he please his parents or would he please the Lord? Thank God, the love of Christ captured him, so that he finally was baptized by immersion.

JULY 18th

No man can say, Jesus is Lord, but in the Holy Spirit. 1 Corinthians 12.3.

We know that there is one declaration God loves to hear from us, which is, that we say to Him, "You Are." And we say to the Lord, "You are Lord!" This important word, that "Jesus is Lord!", can be a most powerful declaration. Sometimes when things are in disarray and Satan mocks you by saying that you are now helpless, all you need do — even if you cannot pray at such a time — is simply to declare. You proclaim aloud: "Jesus is Lord!" And you shall instantly see that entangled things are nothing and that Satan's mocking is nothing. When you are being severely tried, you should rise up and speak this word. Whether it is in your own room or in a prayer meeting, you should say, "Jesus is Lord!" — by which you are telling Him: "You Are!" The Lord loves to hear such a declaration, and we shall be strengthened inwardly as a result.

JULY 19th

Jesus answered and said unto them, Go and tell John the things which ye hear and see ... And blessed is he, whosoever shall find no occasion of stumbling in me. Matthew 11.4, 6.

John the Baptist is offended at not finding the Lord doing things according to his own wish. Blessed is the man who is not offended at what the Lord has appointed him, because not being content with the will of God is a major cause of falling. John does not doubt the Lord, he is only unhappy with the way God has arranged things for him: this is the reason for his fall. In His reply, the Lord gives some hint to John so as to bring him to the knowledge of his own fault. What the Lord answers is nothing but what John has himself heard and seen before. But He adds one important word: "Blessed is he whosoever shall find no occasion of stumbling in me."

JULY 20th

And they that were ready went in with him to the marriage feast . . . Watch therefore, for ye know not the day nor the hour. Matthew 25.10, 13.

To be "ready" means that there is no unfinished business, and one is therefore ready to be reckoned with daily. To "watch" means to so live as to be always ready for the coming of the Lord. We believers should daily be prepared for reckoning. The Lord may come at any time. The five foolish virgins were ready and watching at the beginning, but alas, they did not continue on.

To be ready and watchful and waiting, we need the fullness of the Holy Spirit. It will not do if we depend on ourselves, for very soon we will be weakened and become foolish. But if we are filled with the Holy Spirit, we will spontaneously bear fruit to the glory of God. He who is truly watchful often feels he is not yet entirely ready. He does not trust in his own self. This is true humility.

JULY 21st

And thou shalt love the Lord thy God with all thy heart, and with all thy soul, and with all thy mind, and with all thy strength. Mark 12.30.

By faith life is received; through love life is released. Faith alone will let life in; love alone will let it out.

We must therefore allow this love to reach into our heart. Let us lift up our heart and say: "My God, I will love You with my soul, I will love You with my understanding, I will love you with my strength." Whosoever says this truthfully will soon see that his thought is changed, his speech is changed, his conduct is changed—all within and without him is changed. And why? Because there is the "story of love" within him. Oh, what God expects of us today is that our heart may be touched by Him; that our soul, our understanding, and our strength may all be touched by Him. "But whensoever it [the heart] shall turn to the Lord, the veil is taken away" (2 Cor. 3.16).

JULY 22nd

I am . . . the Living one; and I was dead, and behold, I am alive for evermore. Revelation 1.17, 18.

Knowing the Lord Jesus as the God who lives forever enables us to sense the presence of the Lord unceasingly in our spirit. Nothing strengthens us more than this sense of the Lord's actual presence. One has told the following story concerning the greatest religious reformer in Germany: "Once Martin Luther felt that his future was full of dangers, and hence his heart was filled with sorrow and fear. He knew at the time that unless he could lay hold of the power from on high, he would not be able to get through. As Luther sat alone in his room, he used his finger to draw these words on the table: 'He is alive for evermore!' God is alive! Luther became joyful and his faith was restored."

"He is alive for evermore" is always our strength and our hope. People will all pass away, yet only He exists forever.

JULY 23rd

Whosoever therefore shall humble himself as this little
child, the same is the greatest in the kingdom of heaven.
Matthew 18.4.

The humility shown here relates to the matter of
attitude. We should have a humble attitude. A little child
does not look at himself, nor does he possess a competitive
heart. Paul acknowledges himself as being the least of the
apostles (1 Cor. 15.9)—and this is not determined through
comparison. He would even rather be separated from
Christ if necessary, for the sake of his kinsmen's salvation
(Rom. 9.3). All this reflects how selfless he is. He does not
look at himself at all. Humility is having no pride, not a
having no ability to preach or lead a revival campaign. Only
he who humbles himself as a little child has no pride at all.
And the one who humbles himself shall be exalted.

JULY 24th

Lay thou thy treasure in the dust, . . . and the Almighty
will be thy treasure. Job 22.24, 25.

Generally speaking, believers seem to have finan-
cial difficulties. This is due either to their inability to continue on with whatever improper occupations they had
engaged in before or to some spiritual reason for which
God is dealing with them specifically. God sometimes takes
our wealth away so as to induce us to seek after Christ that
He might have the preeminence in all things. It is not *impossible* for the rich to enter the kingdom of God, it is just
difficult for them to do so.

God dealt with the children of Israel in the wilderness

by depriving them of earthly supplies of food and clothing so that they might recognize the abundance of God. As the supplies on earth ceased, the supplies from heaven came. Material difficulties drive us to seek after the Lord, to learn the lesson of faith, and know Christ as the first in all things.

JULY 25th

My little children, of whom I am again in travail until Christ be formed in you. Galatians 4.19.

Paul was not using empty words here, nor was he expressing sorrow for himself. No, but he was "again in travail" for them. This requires time, love, intercession, tears, and daily expectation.

How many of God's children today have Christ formed in them? How many of those who serve the Lord are so concerned with the spiritual condition of God's children that they are going through this kind of spiritual travail? Alas, it is here that we need to repent, to moan, and to shed tears for our own abnormal condition and for the lack of love towards the children of God. How the spiritual condition of some of His children is so babyish, so abnormal, even backward. Shall the responsibility be fully put upon them? Have we moaned for them and prayed for them? Oh God, forgive us, have mercy upon us!

JULY 26th

Concerning this thing I besought the Lord thrice, that it might depart from me. 2 Corinthians 12.8.

There is one particular secret about prayer that we should know about, which is, a praying three times to the Lord. This "thrice" is not limited to only three times, it may be many times. The Lord Jesus asked God three times in the garden of Gethsemane until His prayer was heard — at which point He stopped. Paul too prayed to God three times, and ceased praying after he was given God's word. Hence all prayers should heed the principle of thrice. This "thrice" does not mean that we need only pray once, twice, and three times, and then stop. It simply signifies the fact that before we stop we must pray thoroughly until God hears us.

JULY 27th

And the women sang one to another as they played, and said, Saul hath slain his thousands, And David his ten thousands. 1 Samuel 18.7.

After David killed Goliath he was put into a peculiar situation by God — for the women of Israel subsequently sang: "Saul hath slain his thousands, and David his ten thousands." Concerning these two clauses, it will be seen that the one was to test David and the other was to test Saul. It is said in Proverbs 27 that "a man is tried by his praise" (v.21). When people overly-praise you, closely notice whether you become proud; or if people under-praise you, watch whether you become jealous. How did these two declarations of the Israelitish women affect the hearts of David and Saul? We learn that David was not at all swayed by the shout, "He hath slain his ten thousands"; Saul, however, was touched deeply by the words that he had only slain his thousands.

JULY 28th

Jesus saith unto her, Mary. She turneth herself, and saith unto him in Hebrew, Rabboni; which is to say, Teacher. John 20.16.

Have we ever heard this voice that Mary heard? If we ever hear this voice—"Mary"—when we pray in our closet, we shall be satisfied. As soon as the Lord said "Mary," she recognized Him right away. This is a revelation. It is enough if the Lord would say but one word. As the shepherd calls his sheep, the eyes of the sheep open immediately. When Mary heard the Lord's voice, she knew instantly that this was not the gardener, but the Teacher. She therefore had no need to weep any more. Whenever the Lord reveals himself to a person, no further words need to be said. Do we, like Mary, recognize the voice of our Lord?

JULY 29th

So belief cometh of hearing, and hearing by the word of Christ. Romans 10.17.

When you have problems with your home, school, business or personal needs, your prayers will be in vain if you do not believe God's word. You have not, because you pray not. You pray and still have not, because you do not believe in God's word (cf. James 4.2, 3). It is a waste of time to pray without believing in the word of God. In order to receive God's grace, one thing which is so necessary is to lay hold of His word. You believe and God performs. Whenever something confronts you, you must ask Him to give you a word. And then with His word, you shall be able to break through any problem whatsoever. To have God's word in such a manner is to possess the sword of the Spirit. Almost all the armor mentioned in Ephesians 6 is for defensive purposes; only the sword of the Holy Spirit, "which is the word of God," is for offensive use. Having God's word, you can overthrow every obstacle and solve all problems.

JULY 30th

Now there went with him great multitudes: and he turned, and said unto them . . . Luke 14.25.

Why are there such great multitudes going with the Lord? Because He has just preached the gospel. As is indicated in the parable which precedes this verse, He invites a great number of people to come. In fact, all who want to eat have come. Many are the Christians; how very joyous it is to be saved. How good it is to be born again and thus to possess the grace of God. These people go along with the Lord, and to them He turns to speak. The purport of what He will next say is this: Yes, you are saved; but if you want to follow Me, you will now have to fulfill certain conditions. He thus raises the standard of truth, for He will not lower God's ordained yardstick on account of the great multitudes. The door by which to believe in the Lord Jesus and to be saved is wide, but the door by which to follow Him and to be glorified with Him is narrow.

JULY 31st

For the word of God is living, . . . piercing even to the dividing of soul and spirit, of both joints and marrow, and quick to discern the thoughts and intents of the heart. Hebrews 4.12.

We ought to acknowledge that it is not easy for us ourselves to differentiate between what is spiritual and what is soulish merely by their outward appearances. It is futile to ask ourselves daily whether this is spiritual or that is soulish. Such questioning will have no spiritual value at all. We may ask, but we will not get an answer. In spiritual things, self-analysis will not only fail to show us the reality, it will even create spiritual paralysis. Real seeing and understanding comes only from God's illumination. As light shines, we just naturally see. We therefore do not need to ask ourselves questions; all we need to do is to ask God to cause his word to shine in us, for the word of God is living and most effective.

AUGUST 1st

So then, my beloved, even as ye have always obeyed, not as in my presence only, but now much more in my absence, work out your own salvation with fear and trembling. Philippians 2.12.

Working out our own salvation with fear and trembling is something for which we ourselves must take responsibility. If we do not take the responsibility, we shall be lopsided in our Christian life. Christ has indeed died for us, shed His blood for us, been resurrected and ascended for us. Yet some people infer from this that such being the case, they have nothing to do but to worship. And thus they become absolutely passive. They feel no need for prayer or Bible reading or consecration. Let it be known, however, that since God has done all for us, we need to be even more zealous. Because God has already worked in, we must work it out.

AUGUST 2nd

And Jehovah spake unto Moses, saying, Sanctify unto me all the first-born, . . . both of man and of beast: it is mine. Exodus 13.1, 2.

Here we are told that hereafter all the first-born of Israel belonged to God. Similarly today, *all who have been bought with the precious blood of the Lamb are God's*. We have been purchased, and therefore we have no liberty. Who may say from their hearts, "God, I belong to You, I am Your slave"? "For ye were bought with a price: glorify God therefore in your body" (1 Cor. 6.20). The day a person is saved is the day that he has been purchased. A slave is purchased with money, whereas a servant is hired for money. One who is *bought* has no liberty to himself at all, but one who is *hired* does have liberty. We are God's bond-slaves, not God's servants. According to the original language of the Bible, we are God's bought slaves and not God's hired servants.

AUGUST 3rd

It is the spirit that giveth life; the flesh profiteth nothing; the words that I have spoken unto you are spirit, and are life. John 6.63.

As we view the work of the Lord Jesus *in* the Holy Spirit we find that all His works are living to us. If we look at His work *outside* the Holy Spirit, all will be mere letters, and letters are dead. If we treat these matters as simply doctrines, they are dead. Some people say that they do believe in the facts recorded in the Bible, but why are these facts not effective in their lives? Others say that they have heard the doctrine, yet they do not find the power. Still others may say that they have found in the Bible God's word, but why does it not work? All these failures are because they do not touch the fact of God *in* the Holy Spirit. For all the things in Christ, if treated as letters or doctrines, become things of the past; if they are approached in the Holy Spirit, however, they never become something past but are always present living realities.

AUGUST 4th

If I by the Spirit of God cast out demons, then is the kingdom of God come upon you. Matthew 12.28.

The kingdom of God is the sovereignty of God. Where His sovereignty is, demons have no power. The Bible speaks of two things: the kingdom of God and the power of God. The kingdom of God represents God's sovereignty. The Spirit of God represents God's power. God has authority because there is power behind it. The Holy Spirit is the power of the kingdom of God. How does the kingdom of God come? Through its power. The Lord manifests power here, so there comes the kingdom of God.

AUGUST 5th

Take my yoke upon you, and learn of me; for I am meek and lowly in heart: and ye shall find rest unto your souls. Matthew 11.29.

Sometimes God puts a careful person and a careless person together, or a strong person and a weak person together, or a healthy person and a sick person together, or a clever person and an ignorant person together, or a quick-tempered person and a slow-tempered person together, or a tidy person and a sloppy person together. So that one will be the yoke to the other, and vice versa. This gives them both the opportunity to learn the nature of Christ. And if you struggle against it, you will have no rest. But if you say to God, "I will take up the yoke You give me, I am willing to take my place, I am willing to obey," you will find rest and joy.

AUGUST 6th

His mother saith unto the servants, Whatsoever he saith unto you, do it. John 2.5.

What matters most to a servant of Christ is to know what God wants him to do, and at what time and by what means. One who serves the Lord has absolutely no need to design his work. One of the characteristics of the New Covenant is that everyone may know God's will. A servant of Christ may receive in his spirit the revelation of the Holy Spirit, thus discerning clearly what God requires of him. Such knowledge is real; it comes neither from his imagination nor from the encouragement or direction of other people. It is based on the teaching of the letter of the Bible and revealed as God's command in the deepest recess of his being by the Holy Spirit who dwells in his spirit.

AUGUST 7th

Always bearing about in the body the dying of Jesus, that the life also of Jesus may be manifested in our body.
2 Corinthians 4.10.

Since we are channels of life, we must not be blocked by anything lest, like water that is clogged in its channel, the life of God cannot pass through us. The work of the cross is to open us up—to rid us of all that belongs to Adam and the natural order so that others may receive the life of the Holy Spirit. By being filled with the Holy Spirit, our spirit is able to bear the cross of Christ continuously. And once filled with the Holy Spirit and possessing the life of the cross, we will then be used by God's Spirit to have issued from us that life of the cross to the people around us. We will spontaneously diffuse life in our conversation and our talk—whether private or public—so as to enrich those with whom we have contact.

AUGUST 8th

And raised us up with him, and made us to sit with him in the heavenly places, in Christ Jesus. Ephesians 2.6.

I recall when I first began to serve the Lord that I prayed He would raise me up with Him. I thought at the time that if the Lord should raise me up with Him I would then have the power to do God's will. It was wrong for me to pray like this, for I had started from myself. All real beginnings lie with Christ. The Bible says that I have been raised with Christ. This is an accomplished fact. Remember that the more we turn in to look at ourselves, the worse we become.

Now I can say, "Lord, I thank You for You have already risen, and I have been raised with You." We need first to believe the fact that I am raised from the dead. Yet how am I raised? Is it because *I feel* I am resurrected? No, it is Christ who has raised me up.

AUGUST 9th

Jehovah will support him upon the couch of languishing: thou makest all his bed in his sickness. Psalm 41.3.

God permits us to be sick and weak in body that we may learn to (1) pray in the night, (2) watch as the sparrow on the housetop, (3) know how the Lord makes our bed, (4) deal with sins, (5) wait in stillness, (6) touch the hem of the Lord's garment, (7) realize how God sends His word to heal us, (8) discern how God uses sickness to make us useful vessels, (9) understand that holiness is healing, and (10) experience the power of the Lord's resurrection in overcoming our weakness, sickness and death. God causes us to learn through sickness how to believe, trust, and obey so that Christ can have the preeminence in our lives.

AUGUST 10th

See ye not all these things? verily I say unto you, There shall not be left here one stone upon another that shall not be thrown down. Matthew 24.2.

Why does the Lord say here that such a beautiful temple will be left desolate to the children of Israel? Simply because the glory of the temple is not in gold, silver and treasures, but in the presence of the Lord. If the Lord is gone, what use is the temple with its gold and treasures of the world? And hence these things ought not be left behind for us to contemplate. Let us, as God's temple, be careful as to whether we have the presence of God or are merely maintaining an outward appearance.

AUGUST 11th

Ask, and it shall be given you; seek and ye shall find; knock, and it shall be opened unto you. Matthew 7.7.

What is the use of praying? Is not God omniscient as well as omnipotent? Why must He wait till we pray before He commences to work? Since He knows, why must we tell Him everything (Phil. 4.6)? Being almighty, why does God not work directly?

By asking these questions we come to realize that prayer *is* a great mystery. For here we see a principle of God's working, which is, that God's people must pray before God himself will rise up and work: His will is only to be realized through the prayers of those who belong to Him: the prayers of the believers are to accomplish His will: God will not fulfill His will alone — He will perform only after His people show their sympathy in prayers.

AUGUST 12th

And he said unto him, I am Jehovah that brought thee out of Ur of the Chaldees, to give thee this land to inherit it. Genesis 15.7.

Did Abraham believe in this promise? His capacity was too small. He voiced his doubt by asking, "O Lord Jehovah, whereby shall I know that I shall inherit it?" This promise was too big for Abraham's faith to apprehend, so he asked God for a proof to seize upon.

Making a covenant was therefore God's way of expanding Abraham's faith. He not only promised but also covenanted with Abraham as to what He would do (v.18). Thus did He cause Abraham to believe. For having established a covenant, God could not help but perform according to His covenant; otherwise, He would be unfaithful, unrighteous, and unlawful. Under the security of such a covenant, Abraham's capacity for faith was naturally enlarged.

AUGUST 13th

There is one body, and one Spirit, even as also ye were
called in one hope of your calling. Ephesians 4.4.

Experience tells us that due to physical weakness or some other cause we cannot avoid having a day or two in the year wherein we are unable to pray and read the Bible as we should. Is it because of such deficiency that I must therefore be defeated? that I must fall to the ground? No, not at all. For most surprisingly, within a given week, say on Monday of that week, I may feel rather near to God, and from Tuesday to Friday I continue to feel all right, but that on Saturday I neither pray nor read the Bible as I should – due probably to fatigue: yet I do not necesarily fall on Saturday, nor need I be worse than Friday; for strangely enough, a power seems to sustain me and bring me through the day. Now what is the cause for such support? Is it not due to the supply of the life of the body of Christ? Unknown to others, some member in the body is praying, asking God to give grace to all His children. And hence life flows from another member to us, thus enabling us to stand.

AUGUST 14th

And being found in fashion as a man, he humbled
himself, becoming obedient even unto death, yea, the
death of the cross. Philippians 2.8.

All who know God as God will learn to be men. For in the fall we were tempted to be gods, but in deliverance we are ready to be humans. The principle of the Garden of Eden is ever that by eating the fruit of the tree of the knowledge of good and evil "ye shall be as gods" (Gen. 3.5 mg.); while the principle of Calvary is to restore us to the position of man.

The purpose of our Lord's birth into a carpenter's home is to be man. His receiving the baptism of John the Baptist is likewise to be man. And He thrice resisted the temptation of the devil, again in order to be man (Matt. 4.1-10). The fact that the Lord "himself hath suffered being tempted" (Heb. 2.18) shows that He is man. If all these are true of our Lord, how much more ought we to be men!

AUGUST 15th

Yea, though I walk through the valley of the shadow of death, I will fear no evil; for thou art with me. Psalm 23.4.

Is there any Christian who can say that his joy to-day exceeds that of the first day on which he was saved? How we believers are troubled in our hearts! We feel we have sinned and are defeated. We do not have as much joy as at the time of our initial salvation. But as a matter of fact, dryness of heart does not *necessarily* mean spiritual ebb.

Allow me to illustrate this point as follows: When I find my lost watch, I feel most happy. A few days later, however, my joy will not be as buoyant as when I first found my watch. And perhaps within a few more days, this joy has completely faded away. Yet at that moment my watch has not been lost again. What has happened here? Simply this, that what is now lost is not my watch once again but the joy at finding the watch in the first place! Here is what we all need to recognize; namely, that although the believer's joyful feeling has been lost, the object of that joy has not been lost.

AUGUST 16th

Verily, verily, I say unto you, Except a grain of wheat fall into the earth and die, it abideth by itself alone; but if it die, it beareth much fruit. John 12.24.

Here the Lord Jesus reveals the principle of fruit bearing: the grain of wheat which is sown must first *die* before it will bear much fruit. Hence death is the indispensable process for fruit bearing. The fact of the matter is, death *is* the only way to bear fruit. How we ask the Lord for greater power that we may bear more fruit; but the Lord tells us that we need to die, that we must have the experience of the cross if we desire the power of the Holy Spirit. Frequently in our attempt to achieve Pentecost we bypass Calvary, not realizing that without our being crucified and thus losing all belonging to the natural, the Holy Spirit cannot work with us to gain many people. Here is the spiritual principle: die, and *then* bear fruit.

AUGUST 17th

I acknowledged my sin unto thee, and mine iniquity did I not hide. Psalm 32.5.

How many feel sorrowful after they have sinned? If people do not feel sorrowful, this indicates that they have failed in the matter of confessing sin. But if any Christian will clear up his sins against God and men with confession, he will proceed well in the course which is before him. He will walk faster than other Christians. How sad that many believers have too little sensitivity toward sin. I am surprised at finding people sleeping soundly and eating well after they have committed sins. Our God hates sin. I hate sin not because of saving face or fear of its consequence, but because of God. In order to sharpen their sensitivity toward sin, let Christians confess their sins. I can say at the very least that confessing sin will help us to hate sin.

AUGUST 18th

Wherein God, being minded to show more abundantly unto the heirs of the promise the immutability of his counsel, interposed with an oath. Hebrews 6.17.

The Scriptures show us that God's covenant is God's promise; except that God's promise is what He says whereas God's covenant is further interposed with an oath. If promise is binding to God, covenant is much more binding.

To those who have been deeply taught by God's grace and who know Him well, God's promise and God's covenant do not make much difference; for they know He is as faithful as He is righteous. They believe that once God has promised, it shall be done. There is no need for His promises to be put into legal form. They look upon God's promise as being just as good as His covenant. But to those whose faith is weak, God's covenant is quite different from His promise, in that covenant seems to guarantee the fulfillment of promise.

AUGUST 19th

*And God saw everything that he had made, and, behold,
it was very good.* Genesis 1.31.

God never made anything bad. All things bad
come from sin and not from God's creation. We who live
in this evil world should not murmur against God, because
in Him there is no evil and nothing bad ever came from His
creative hands. On the contrary, God treated mankind with
utmost kindness. He prepared the grass and herbs on the
third day as food for man. He made ready the environment
before He put us in it. If we truly see this touch of kindness,
what comfort it can be to us! God always provides for His
creatures. Before the grass, He prepared the earth; before
the animals, He prepared the plants. Sometimes we grow
fearful because we fail to see God and His goodness. But
how blessed are those with faith! For nothing can shake
their hearts!

AUGUST 20th

*Wherefore let him that thinketh he standeth take heed
lest he fall.* 1 Corinthians 10.12.

Let me tell you that except by leaning on God and
trusting Him moment by moment, I do not know of any
way to live a sanctified life. If we do not rely on the Lord
we will not know how long we may continue with Him.
Without depending on God we can do nothing, not even
can we live as Christians for a single day. Do we really feel
this way now? Were it not for His grace we would be

defeated on every side. We need to continue to prostrate ourselves before Him in fear and trembling, and to seek for His grace.

AUGUST 21st

And gave him [Christ] to be head over all things to the church. Ephesians 1.22.

Have you ever said to the Lord: "O Lord, You are my head. I have no right to decide anything, nor have I authority to make any choice of my own. May You deliver me from trying to be head." Each one of us needs to learn how to accept the command of God: Christ is head, and therefore no one can follow his own will. To be subdued by the Lord and then to capitulate to Him should be a basic experience of every Christian.

Take a look at the experience of Paul at his conversion. While he was on the way to Damascus the Lord shone around him. And then he asked: "Who art thou, Lord?" (Acts 9.5) Paul first saw Jesus as Lord before he believed on Him as Savior. Oh how we all must come to the place where we can honestly say: "O Lord, I am finished. Henceforth, it is You who directs me, because You are the Lord."

AUGUST 22nd

For I will be merciful to their iniquities, and their sins will I remember no more. Hebrews 8.12.

How regrettable that we often forget what God remembers and remember what God forgets. Some people are always musing: Does God really forgive after I have committed so many grievous sins? Will He indeed remember them no more? Yet others may think that even though God has blotted out sins, the scars which no doubt remain will forever remind God of what a sinner they are.

If anyone is still bothered by his past sins and has no rest in his conscience, let him sing the following hymn till he can respond with an amen in his heart:

> *Why should I worry, doubt and fear?*
> *Has God not caused His Son to bear*
> *My sins upon the tree?*
> *The debt that Christ for me has paid,*
> *Would God another mind have made*
> *To claim again from me?*

AUGUST 23rd

And be not fashioned according to this world: but be ye transformed by the renewing of your mind, that ye may prove what is the good and acceptable and perfect will of God. Romans 12.2.

A renewed mind can actually prove what the good and acceptable and perfect will of God is. How frequently on a given point this thing seems to be God's will but that thing seems also to be His will. How often we mistake one for the other. But a renewed mind will make no mistake concerning the will of God. Unless our mind is renewed, we will not be able to prove what the will of God is. And thus we will not have experienced a full salvation. Yet God has not only saved us to where we are today, He will also save us even further to a perfect position. And it is to this that we must aspire and it is for this that we must thank God.

AUGUST 24th

Which indeed is less than all seeds; but when it is grown,
it is greater than the herbs, and becometh a tree, so that
the birds of the heaven come and lodge in the branches
thereof. Matthew 13.32.

How the church has lost her original quality of depending on God. Like the mustard seed she has become a tree having an enormous outward form, yet she is so lacking in reality.

Let us therefore maintain the appropriate "smallness." Do not admire the greatness of men. In honor prefer one another; in suffering, outdo one another. Let us have the will to suffer. Let our pocket *be* poor if necessary, if only our spirit may be rich. The secret of victory lies in standing on the ground which the Lord has given us. When Saul esteemed himself as small, God used him. But when he became self-important, God sought for another person — David. The person whom the Lord seeks is a small vessel, not a big one.

AUGUST 25th

Besides those things that are without, there is that which
presseth upon me daily, anxiety for all the churches. 2
Corinthians 11.28.

If one or more of the believers are truly humble before the Lord and fear Him, what should they do when they discover problems among His children? They should learn to do one thing: to bear the children of the Lord on their shoulders and carry them in their bosoms as they go to inquire of the Father (cf. Ex. 28). Just as Paul did, who bore on his shoulders all the saints of God and carried in his bosom all the churches of God.

We need to understand how Paul could write so clearly to the churches on the ways of God. None of his letters was written out of some words which suddenly came to him when he prayed casually for the churches. Paul did not write in such a careless way. We must understand and practice this principle of carrying the saints of the Lord to God's presence. We do not know for how many days or weeks Paul might have carried the children of God on his heart as he would look to the Father. But then, one day he saw something in God's light; and with that light he would sit down and write a letter.

AUGUST 26th

That which is born of the flesh is flesh; and that which is born of the Spirit is spirit. John 3.6.

Who truly recognizes what the flesh is? Who understands what is meant by dealing with the flesh? or judging of the flesh? Many people deem victory over sin to be the hallmark of perfection. Yet they do not know that there is the flesh which sins! According to the Scriptures, "the flesh" is condemned by God. It is something with which God is most displeased. The flesh is everything we have through birth.

Whatever we have by birth is of the flesh, and includes not only sin and uncleanness and corruption but also natural goodness, ability, zeal, wisdom and power. A most difficult lesson to be learned in a believer's life is for that one to know his own flesh. The Christian must be brought through all kinds of failures and deprivations before he knows what his flesh is.

AUGUST 27th

*And seeing them distressed in rowing, for the wind was
contrary unto them, about the fourth watch of the night
he cometh unto them.* Mark 6.48.

The period of the fourth watch is obviously the
darkest hour during the entire night and it also brings an
end to the night. Now it is just such a time as this that we
must press on. I well realize that we all have temptations
and trials. Yet the greatest peril today is to cool off a little,
to compromise somewhat, or to take a brief nap—for we
are really tired. At the beginning there was strength to
stand, for we were under the constraint of love. But the in-
tervening period has now become so long and the struggle
has grown so very difficult that it is easy to become cold.

One brother once commented that he rarely sees people
anymore who are still zealous in the Lord's work after fifty
years of age. Cooling off one's ardor and faithfulness
somewhat is a thing harder to overcome than all other
temptations. To overcome sin is possible, but to not become
cold from constant sailing against the wind is almost
impossible.

AUGUST 28th

*Be ye kind one to another, tenderhearted, forgiving each
other, even as God also in Christ forgave you.* Ephesians
4.32.

A brother once said: "If a little brother sins against
me, I can forgive him; but if a big brother sins against me,
I cannot forgive him." Another brother who heard him say
this looked at the chest of this brother and nodded his head

continuously. What he meant by this gesture was: "Your heart! Your heart! In forgiving a little brother but not forgiving a big brother, you expose what your heart is like. The fact that a little brother sins against you and is forgiven by you cannot at all expose your true heart condition; but when you refuse to forgive a big brother who sins against you, that really reveals what is in your heart." Through this incident, that brother's unforgiving heart was unveiled.

AUGUST 29th

And Moses said unto Jehovah, Oh, Lord, I am not eloquent, neither heretofore, nor since thou hast spoken unto thy servant; for I am slow of speech, and of a slow tongue. Exodus 4.10.

Knowing one's own uselessness alone is still useless. The important thing is to know the power of God. And this is true resurrection. God had wanted Moses to know that it was He who had made man's mouth. God tried to encourage Moses. "Oh, Lord, send, I pray thee, by the hand of him whom thou wilt send" (Ex. 4.13). Moses again excused himself. When God heard this, He was angry with Moses. And why? Because even though it is of great importance and highly acceptable to God that we are brought to the place of no self-confidence and no self-reliance, nevertheless, if we stay *there* and refuse to go forward by trusting in God, we will greatly displease Him.

How we need to be careful lest we swing from one extreme to the other. God takes us through death in order to raise us up. Death is not the end, resurrection is the goal. We will be of no use if we remain in death and not come into resurrection.

AUGUST 30th

Therefore let us . . . lay aside every weight. Hebrews 12.1.

What is a weight? A weight may not be sin, nor is it necessarily something very bad, but it doubtless can easily entangle us. Anything which keeps us from running well or hinders our progress may be viewed as a weight.

During the nineteenth century there was a man who was greatly used by the Lord. He spent a great deal of time compiling a Hebrew dictionary. Upon finishing the work he sent it to his friends for review. All of them praised the work highly. Yet this brother burned his manuscript. For, when he was compiling it, said the would-be scholar, he felt his love for the Lord as well as his love for souls had been greatly diminished. So that for him, to proofread and to print it would subsequently occupy even more of his time and energy. By taking the action he did take, this believer was delivered from a weight.

AUGUST 31st

Or are ye ignorant that all we who were baptized into Christ Jesus were baptized into his death? Romans 6.3.

When we are baptized we are baptized into Christ—not our merely being baptized in water but being baptized into Christ. According to the last clause in Romans 6.3 ("were baptized into his death"), the water of baptism spoken of in that verse points to death. But according to the first clause of the same verse ("were baptized into Christ Jesus"), the water also refers to Christ. Frequently we look to God for a cup of water. No, God wants us to enter into Christ. If we are clear on this point, we shall know that it is not a matter of we ourselves; it is instead Christ, and all things are in Him.

SEPTEMBER 1st

Forever, O Jehovah, thy word is settled in heaven. Psalm 119.89.

Suppose my father bought some land and gave me the deed to it. He tells me to go and manage this estate. So I go to the country where the land is. I meet a vagabond who asks why I am coming there. "I have come to find my father's land," I reply. "This is not your father's land; it is my father's land," the vagabond protests. Now if I at that moment were to doubt my father's word, I probably would return home. But if I say, "No, no, my father has made no mistake; for according to this title deed in my hand, this land is ours," the vagabond would have to go away. Hence, it is either he or I who must go.

Now with us, it is the same way. For God the Father has already given you all blessings in Christ Jesus. And the Bible is the title deed which the Father gives you. If you believe what is written in the Bible, Satan will have to go.

SEPTEMBER 2nd

For they loved the glory that is of men more than the glory that is of God. John 12.43.

Ever since man ate the fruit of the tree of the knowledge of good and evil, the glory of men has become a basic problem in the soul of man. Each one of us has his own throne, and this throne is built on the glory of men. Yet if we would desire to be faithful servants of the Lord, we must come down from our thrones. Otherwise, we will not be able to serve our Lord. Hebrews 12.2 tells us that our Lord Jesus endured the cross, despising shame. He willingly chose the cross. And the cross is not only death, it is also shame. If you have ever truly been broken by the cross, there will be for you a clear experience of having despised shame. May God be gracious to us in causing us to have a heart to please the Lord, that by His grace we may be faithful servants.

SEPTEMBER 3rd

So then each one of us shall give account of himself to God. Romans 14.12.

All failures and sins throughout our lives which have passed under the blood and been dealt with on the cross will not be judged at the judgment seat. Indeed, at this seat the Lord will only judge our undealt-with idle words, thoughts, and works. As penetrating as the light of the judgment seat may be, it can never uncover sins which are already under the blood. How then do we deal, for example, with the tongue which often delights to indulge in idle words? We need the cross. And the same is true with our unprofitable thoughts and works. They too need the cross. Let us therefore accept the cross by faith, reckon that this old man was crucified on the cross, and then the judgment seat can never search out for judgment those things in our lives that have already been dealt with by the cross.

SEPTEMBER 4th

In praying use not vain repetitions, as the Gentiles do: for they think that they shall be heard for their much speaking. Matthew 6.7.

"Repetitions" means using many meaningless words to prolong prayer. This in no sense forbids the use of the same words in prayer. Even the Lord Jesus prayed three times in the same words; hence it shows that when there is burden in the spirit, the same words are frequently uttered in His many prayers. Those who know best how to pray are rather creative in their prayers.

There is a poor habit among us believers today. We tend to pray long prayers, stretching out our prayers with many words and so thinking that we shall be heard for much speaking. However, prayers recorded in the Bible are most straightforward and concise. For example, "Save, Lord" (Matt. 8.25). A very short prayer is often quite acceptable. In a time of distress, in witnessing to a sinner, in an hour of need, short prayers are most effective.

SEPTEMBER 5th

Jesus answered and said unto her, If thou knewest the gift of God, and who it is that saith to thee, Give me to drink; thou wouldest have asked of him, and he would have given thee living water. John 4.10.

God never sells anything. "Gift" means something freely given. God always gives freely to men. And He will give to whoever asks. God gives us sunlight without charge; He gives us rainfall without cost. He will also give you spiritual satisfaction in exactly the same fashion.

Once there was a child who loved his mother dearly. He thought of buying some flowers to please her heart. He had only two pennies in his pocket. That day he saw a most beautiful garden, and entered it thinking of buying some flowers. A gentleman was there to whom he expressed his wish. So the gentleman picked some flowers and handed them to him. The boy politely said that he could not take the flowers without paying. But the man replied: "My flowers are always given freely. If you want them, I will give them to you." Who was that man? He was the Prince of Wales, and this was the royal garden. *Royal* things are never for sale.

SEPTEMBER 6th

Thy word is a lamp unto my feet, and light unto my path. Psalm 119.105.

When our spiritual condition is normal we are as though walking under blue sky and bright sun. But our spiritual condition does not always remain constant. The Bible says that "thy word is a lamp unto my feet, and light unto my path." Were there no dark night there would be no need of lamp or light. When we are bright inwardly, our inner sensation is clear and sure; but when we are inwardly dark, our inner sensation tends to be confused and flickering; and so there is the need to check with the word of the Scriptures. Life plus truth becomes real and steady power. We must walk on this lasting path of both life *and* truth. Every thought and judgment of ours needs to have checked against it the word of the Bible. This will help us to walk straight ahead without turning to the left or right.

SEPTEMBER 7th

Giving thanks unto the Father, . . . who delivered us out of the power of darkness, and translated us into the kingdom of the Son of his love. Colossians 1.12, 13.

Indeed, God wants to bless us; but He desires even more greatly for us to enter His kingdom and to be *under His government*. Oh let us all realize that salvation is not merely for enjoyment; it is preeminently to be placed under the sovereignty of God. Formerly we did what we liked and wasted away our days carelessly; now we are required to submit to God. Once we are saved we cannot afford to be careless. We must accept disciplines. Salvation is none other than being put under the yoke of the Holy Spirit. If anyone wants to be saved, the Holy Spirit will place a yoke on that one. And whoever has this yoke upon him or her is saved. From the standpoint of the flesh, salvation is not at all pleasant because it brings the person under the sovereignty and government of God.

SEPTEMBER 8th

And when the disciples heard it, they fell on their face, and were sore afraid. And Jesus came and touched them and said, Arise, and be not afraid. And lifting up their eyes, they saw no one, save Jesus only. Matthew 17.6-8.

"Sore afraid"—Who is not afraid when God appears!

"Be not afraid"—This occus 365 times in the Bible; one can be appropriated for each day of the year. Every day can be blessed "now"; for this is still the dispensation of Grace.

"They saw no one, save Jesus only"—The law and the

prophets, the glory of the Son of man, the overshadowing of a bright cloud and the Voice, as well as the companions: all have passed away: Jesus alone remains. May we see Jesus only.

SEPTEMBER 9th

May grow up in all things into him, who is the head, even Christ; from whom all the body fitly framed and knit together. Ephesians 4.15, 16.

From this passage we learn that the members of the body of Christ are fitly framed and knit together because all hold fast the head and live out the life of the body. This does not suggest that God wants you to pay attention only to the one who sits next to you, but that He preeminently wants you to have a proper relationship with the Lord. If you maintain such a relationship with the head you will have a good relationship with other body members. All matters between you and your brothers and sisters may be easily solved if you can submit yourself to the head. If you have no controversy with the Lord you will have no problem with any brother or sister.

SEPTEMBER 10th

Jesus answered, Verily, verily, I say unto thee, Except one be born of water and the Spirit, he cannot enter into the kingdom of God. John 3.5.

The baptism of repentance in which John baptized with water could not regenerate people. Except one be born "of water and the Spirit" he is not born again. The baptism of repentance announces that not only man's behavior—being deadly wicked—needs to be repented of, but also man himself—being corrupted and dead—must be buried in baptism.

Yet man is not born again "of water" alone; he must be born both "of water *and* the Spirit." He must receive the gift of the Holy Spirit from the Lord Jesus before he can have God's life. Repentance delivers us from all which belongs to us. Believing gets us into all which belongs to God. We enter the water through repentance, we receive the Holy Spirit by faith. This is regeneration.

SEPTEMBER 11th

Remember Lot's wife. Whosoever shall seek to gain his life shall lose it: but whosoever shall lose his life shall preserve it. I say unto you, In that night there shall be two men on one bed; the one shall be taken, and the other shall be left. Luke 17.32-4.

There does not appear to be any difference between the two persons, neither in work nor in place; yet in rapture there does come a difference! In a twinkling, what a *vast* difference!

A most serious problem is presented here. If we wish to be raptured, to see the Lord, and to enter the kingdom, we must first lose our souls in this age. For the sake of the Lord, we must forsake the world, forsake all which is not in accordance with the will of God, forsake all which will entangle us, and forsake all that would hinder our hearts from thinking on the things above. Should we be like Lot's wife, trying to preserve the soul and unwilling to forsake anything, we will not be taken up to where the Lord ordains us to be, even though we may not perish in Sodom and Gomorrah with the sinners. There may be no difference in eternal life, but there *will* be a difference in rapture.

SEPTEMBER 12th

How can one enter into the house of the strong man, and spoil his goods, except he first bind the strong man? and then he will spoil his house. Matthew 12.29.

Binding the strong man is done through the Spirit of God. The power of the Holy Spirit is needed in casting out demons. They are cast out in the name of the Lord because the Holy Spirit is the power of that Name.

How is the strong man bound? Indirectly through the cross of our Lord Jesus. On the cross the Lord has crushed the head of Satan (see Gen. 3.15). The cross has dealt with Satan's head, that is, it has destroyed his power and influence. But after our Lord arose from the dead and ascended back to heaven, the Holy Spirit came to earth to execute what the Lord had accomplished on the cross. Hence binding Satan is done through the power of the Holy Spirit on the basis of the cross. On our side, we can bind Satan through the prayer of faith. We should use prayer to bind the strong man. One great principle in the Lord's work, then, is first to bind and next to spoil.

SEPTEMBER 13th

Ye serve the Lord Christ. Colossians 3.24.

Serving God and working for God are vastly different. Many work for God, but they are not serving Him. Faithful works — if they are really for Christ — are judged by motive and purpose. We must not labor for our own increase, for our own group, or even for our own pet teaching; we ought to work solely for Christ. We rejoice if God can gain something. We are glad whenever He has something to gain even though it does not come from our work. We are not out to save our teaching but to save sinners. Not out to gratify our own heart, simply to satisfy the heart of Christ.

SEPTEMBER 14th

But we all, with unveiled face beholding as in a mirror the glory of the Lord, are transformed into the same image from glory to glory, even as from the Lord the Spirit. 2 Corinthians 3.18.

A coppersmith pours the liquid copper into a mold, and thus the copper poured in takes on the form of the mold. Or take the example of cake making, in which a man puts a prepared dough into a mold resulting in the cake taking upon itself the form of the mold. We are to be likened to the Lord to just that extent! To the extent of being "conformed to the image of his Son" as Paul says in Romans 8.29. It means we are to be like the Lord in His glorified manhood. If man is to be really changed according to the pattern set by God, he must undergo a transformation in inner quality; that is, he must have the life of

God coming into his spirit and must allow it to permeate his whole being till through the change of nature he arrives at the total transformation of image. The Spirit of the Lord works step by step; it is "from glory to glory." Praise the Lord!

SEPTEMBER 15th

Why art thou cast down, O my soul? And why art thou disquieted within me? Hope thou in God; for I shall yet praise him, who is the help of my countenance, and my God. Psalm 42.11.

Many Christians live too much by feeling. If they feel joyful and happy today they will say God has truly blessed them. If, however, they feel cold and flat today they each will almost be heard to say, How can I know where God is? Thus many Christians lean upon their feeling; and as soon as their feeling is missing, they waver. This proves that they do not really know the Lord. How the children of God need to be brought by the Lord to the place where feeling cold or warm, flat or stirred, presents no problem because they have known God with a knowledge which is deeper than any feeling. In spite of varied sensations outwardly—whether of joy or pain—they inwardly know. And only such persons as these can stand against all shakings.

SEPTEMBER 16th

*Unto one he gave five talents, to another two, to another
one; to each according to his several ability; and he went
on his journey.* Matthew 25.15.

There is no ground for pride and satisfaction to the
ones who receive five and two talents, respectively; nor, on
the other hand, is there any reason for shame and envy by
the one who only receives one talent. How believers in the
church today esteem the more and despise the less! All this
is the activity of the flesh.

He who receives but one talent has the greatest temptation. He tends to bury his gift and grow lazy. He is ashamed
of the little he has been given; he is also conscious of how
little he can earn from it by trading. So that he simply
buries his gift in the earth. Though he cannot preach a
great sermon and save several hundred people at one time,
though he is unable to do such spectacular work, he can
still do a little something for the Lord. May we be willing
to do a little work if God is willing to give a little gift.

SEPTEMBER 17th

*If anyone sin, and commit a trespass against Jehovah,
and . . . have found that which was lost, and deal falsely
therein.* Leviticus 6.2, 3.

Though we may not take this matter seriously, it is
nonetheless a tresspass. We may speculate that there is
nothing unrighteous in picking up what is lost. Still God
declares that it is a false dealing. No Christian should take
as his own what belongs to other people. Many have the
idea that it is better for money to fall into their own pockets

than into the pockets of other people. But this is unrighteous thinking. We should not pick up anything and consider it ours, even if it is a handkerchief, a hat, a fountain pen or a letter. For this is unrighteous. We may have done such a thing in the past, but let us try our best to return it. We should either let the one who lost it regain it or deliver the lost item to the local authorities. Otherwise, we have sinned.

SEPTEMBER 18th

And there was a famine in the land, besides the first famine that was in the days of Abraham. Genesis 26.1.

In Egypt there was generally no famine; yet even when it had had such, it had its old grain for relief. In Canaan, however, there seemed to have been frequent famine. This, spiritually speaking, indicates to us that in the world there is little or no famine for the one who is not only in the world but of the world as well; but for the person who is in the way of obedience to God, there will sometimes *be* famine; for by comparison there is little or no trial in the world, whereas in the way of obedience there may be much trial. Yet however great is the trial, with God there is always a living way out (see 1 Cor. 10.13). Hence let us be watchful as well as faithful.

SEPTEMBER 19th

Are not two sparrows sold for a penny? and not one of
them shall fall on the ground without your Father. Matthew 10.29.

The greatest error of our modern age is to pay too much attention to mankind in general while neglecting in particular the individual who is his own self. Not so, though, with God. Although He means to bless mankind, He starts out with the individual. He does not despise any person. "Are not two sparrows sold for a penny? and not one of them shall fall on the ground without your Father." We ought to see the Father's hand in all His works. Man has indeed sinned and fallen, but thank God He does not despise anyone. How He pours out His heart towards every person. And such should be our comfort. Only God's heart can ever truly satisfy man's heart.

SEPTEMBER 20th

Whether therefore ye eat, or drink, or whatsoever ye do,
do all to the glory of God. 1 Corinthians 10.31.

Right or wrong, straight or crooked, spiritually valuable or unvaluable—all these are measured by the presence or absence of God's glory. Certain matters may be minute and insignificant in human eyes, yet at times when you touch these you touch the very glory of God. And as you touch His glory, you know you already have obtained His guidance. You have no need to wait anymore. While doing some works you may sense little worth or that something is not quite right in them, whereas other works you are engaged in make you feel they are worthwhile and in-

trinsically right. The problem lies not in the outward greatness or smallness of the work; it hinges instead upon the
presence or absence of the glory of God: *without* God's
glory, no value; *with* His glory, much value.

SEPTEMBER 21st

*Love not the world, neither the things that are in the
world. If any man love the world, the love of the Father
is not in him.* 1 John 2.15.

Once there was a painting exhibition. One of the
paintings pointed allegorically to a Christian. In the picture
there were lying around all kinds of toys which a child
loved. Yet that child did not seem to notice any of them; his
eyes instead were fixed upon the window before him, and
also his hands were stretched forward. Viewing the painting
from a distance would suggest nothing at all, but a closer
look revealed a beautiful tiny pigeon perched on the window sill. And the caption beneath the painting indicated in
so many words that for the sake of wanting that pretty little
pigeon the child forsook all the toys. And thus the moral
of the picture became obvious: that in order to possess the
more excellent thing one must leave the other things. God
has not demanded that we cast away anything; He instead
puts before us the more excellent. For the sake of possessing
the more excellent, we naturally will forsake many lesser
things.

SEPTEMBER 22nd

Knowing this, that our old man was crucified with him.
Romans 6.6.

It is imperative for us to ask the Spirit of the Lord for revelation that we may see how our old man *was* crucified with Christ. No matter how temptation may sometimes come — causing us to feel as though our old man has not died — we will nonetheless believe in what God has done rather than in our feeling and experience. When we truly see this as a fact we shall find that the experience of it will naturally follow. Let us notice that God's fact does not become factual because we so believe; instead, we believe so because God's fact is already factual.

Whenever he is tempted or tested, the person must believe that God's word and God's fact are more dependable than his own feeling. If he fully believes in God's word, God will be responsible for giving him the experience. Should a person turn to his own past negative experience he will be defeated and will not have any future positive experience. By our believing in God's fact, our spiritual life will daily advance.

SEPTEMBER 23rd

For which of you, desiring to build a tower, does not first sit down and count the cost, whether he have wherewith to complete it? Luke 14.28.

The Lord talks about counting the cost. What He really means to say here is whether a person is willing to put up *all* he has in order to build a tower. For example, if the building of a tower will cost $500 and a man is only willing to put in $300 while keeping his remaining $200 for other purposes, it becomes insufficient only because he keeps a part back. He who keeps back love for others is unable to love Christ. One must hate his own father and mother and wife and children and brothers and sisters — and even his own life — in the sense of taking them out of his heart. Christ does not ask how much a person gives but rather if he has given all to Him.

SEPTEMBER 24th

And they shall see the Son of man coming on the clouds of heaven with power and great glory. Matthew 24.30.

After His first coming, the Lord manifested both great *authority* and glory. At His second coming, He will manifest *power* and glory. At His first coming, people marveled at his teaching and authority (Matt. 7.28). The Pharisees questioned Him as to the source of His authority (21.23). A centurion believed in His authority (8.8-9). But at His second coming, He will not only manifest authority but also power. He will not ride on a colt (as the Prince of Peace) but will ride instead on a white horse. Power is used in executing the judgment of God. Even when He overturned tables and drove out sheep and oxen with a scourge of cords, He did not use the whip on men. Only at His second coming will He exercise such power.

SEPTEMBER 25th

Let us run with patience the race that is set before us.
Hebrews 12.1.

We who are running this race must run "with patience." Why with patience? Because the reward is not given at the start, nor in the middle, but at the very end of the course. Before the end is reached, none can guarantee whether he will be rewarded. One may fail at the last five steps. Once in a 200 meters dash, one man ran ahead of the rest by the distance of about twenty meters through most of the race, but then suddenly fell down with only two meters left to the end. In order to win, a person must be very careful. Before the end is reached no one can boast that he has the reward. Even the apostle Paul must say this: "Not that I have already obtained, or am already made perfect; but I press on" (Phil. 3.12). If such was true of Paul, then what about us?

SEPTEMBER 26th

Looking unto Jesus the author and perfecter of our faith. Hebrews 12.2.

What is meant by looking to Jesus? It is not to look at one's self. To look off to Jesus is to be so attracted by Him that a person leaves his own inner world and is joined to the One to whom he looks. What kind of Jesus do you look to? You look to a Jesus who is both author and perfecter of your faith—the all-inclusive Jesus. The secret of spiritual advance, then, is to know how not to dwell on one's personal condition. He who knows how not to look at himself is truly blessed. May the Spirit of God give us revelation, causing us to know what "looking away" is and how not to have an improper recollection of oneself.

SEPTEMBER 27th

Upon this rock I will build my church; and the gates of Hades shall not prevail against it. Matthew 16.18.

Gates serve as entrance and exit. Neither Hades nor death can hold on to believers or the church, because the incorruptible life has already been manifested in them (see 2 Tim. 1.10). This incorruptible life has come out of Hades. For the Lord has the authority to have His life enter in and exit out of Hades at will. Hades has no power to hold back this life. And what has been deposited in the believer is the very same life. For this reason, Hades cannot withhold us either. However vicious the environment— trial, persecution, malice, murder, and so forth—and though we may be walled in on all sides, we shall have a life which can neither be withheld nor overcome by any environment.

SEPTEMBER 28th

[Christ Jesus] emptied himself, taking the form of a servant, being made in the likeness of men. Philippians 2.7.

This means He accepted limitation. In heaven, our Lord is free to move wherever He wishes. But after He was incarnated and took upon himself the likeness of men, He grew up from babyhood to manhood. He grew according to the age of men, and as man He needed to eat and drink as well as to sleep and rest. This was a tremendous restriction to His deity. Indeed, He became even more limited by taking the form of a bondservant. As a man, He still had the freedom of men as well as experiencing the enjoyment that men have. Now, though, taking the form of a bondservant, He sacrificed even the freedom of an ordinary man. He was restricted and bound in all His ways; He knew nothing except His Father's will. What restriction He must have accepted in His humanity! Though being the infinite God, the Lord Jesus accepted finite limitation; and though He became man, He accepted even further restriction.

SEPTEMBER 29th

The seven stars are the angels of the seven churches: and the seven candlesticks are seven churches. Revelation 1.20.

The first chapter of Revelation tells us that the church is the golden candlestick. God in His word not only says the church is golden, He also says that the church is the golden candlestick. If the church is only golden, she cannot satisfy God's heart. Why does God say the church is the golden *candlestick*? Because the golden candlestick serves the purpose of spreading the light so that the light may shine far and wide. God wants the church to be a shining vessel, a vessel of testimony. From the very beginning He has ordained the church to be a candlestick. Not one certain person, but the entire church. In the divine view the church is a candlestick. It is therefore not enough for it simply to be golden, which means that everything about it is of God; it must also shine for God and testify for Him as the golden candlestick.

SEPTEMBER 30th

Ye search the scriptures, because ye think that in them ye have eternal life; and these are they which bear witness of me; and ye will not come to me, that ye may have life. John 5.39, 40.

If a person receives some religious truth from a book or from a teacher or even from the Bible itself without the need of prayer, of laying down one's power or of depending completely on the Holy Spirit, he is receiving that truth in the power of his mind. For the acceptance of truth in the power of the mind means receiving it directly from a book, teacher or the Bible while by-passing the Holy Spirit. The Pharisees knew the Scriptures directly in this way; hence, what they ended up possessing was something dead, void of any living experience before God—for the word of God leads people to draw nigh to Him, and God himself is Spirit.

OCTOBER 1st

And made us to sit with him in the heavenly places, in Christ Jesus. Ephesians 2.6.

I spent many hours when first believing in the Lord trying to figure out how blessed it would be if I could sit in the heavenly places daily and have sins under my feet. But as with flying an airplane, I could not endure for very long up above. I soon fell down. I prayed and prayed, hoping that one day I could sit securely in the heavenly places and break my old record of ascension. One day as I read Ephesians 2.6 I began to understand. At the time a Christian is raised together with Christ, he is also made to sit with Christ in the heavenly places. He sits there with Christ not because of his diligence or because of his prayer, but because he was taken to the heavenly places at the time Christ himself ascended to heaven. Christ is in the heavenly places, and therefore I too am in the heavenly places.

OCTOBER 2nd

And, behold, there came a man of God out of Judah by the word of Jehovah unto Bethel . . . Now there dwelt an old prophet in Bethel. 1 Kings 13.1, 11.

This old prophet in Bethel was a man who in the past had been used by God, but now he was no longer usable. When God wished to warn Jeroboam because of his sin in Bethel, He did not send the old prophet who lived in Bethel to speak for Him.

The phrase "man of God" denotes that such a one has communion with God, and communion is the basis for light from God. The moment communion stops, at that very moment light ceases. This old prophet once had a spiritual history, for he *was* at one time a prophet; however, he had now lost communion with the Lord. He became an *old* prophet when God could no longer use him. How grave is this situation. In view of this, we must attend to a very important issue in our Christian walk—namely, how not to be set aside by God, how not to be rejected or remain unused. Our freshness before the Lord is a most vital habit to be established or maintained.

OCTOBER 3rd

And what the exceeding greatness of his power to us-ward who believe, according to that working of the strength of his might which he wrought in Christ, when he raised him from the dead. Ephesians 1.19, 20.

Paul *prayed* in his day for the saints in Ephesus that they might see the exceeding greatness of the power which God had already given them. Now if we today do not see that the power in us and the power in Christ is one and the same power, we too must *pray* for seeing. If the power manifested in us is less than the power that was manifested in Christ, we should acknowledge that there are still many things which we have not seen. Let us humbly confess and pray to God to make us see. The power which God works in those who believe is according to the working of the strength of His might which He wrought in Christ. Hallelujah! This is the spiritual fact. Let us ask God to open our eyes that we may truly perceive and understand. We will not ask Him to pour upon us more power from outside; no, we will only ask Him to cause us to discover and to see more that is in us already.

OCTOBER 4th

Why could not we cast it out? And he saith unto them,
Because of your little faith: for verily I say unto you, If
ye have faith as a grain of mustard seed, ye shall say
unto this mountain, Remove hence to yonder place; and
it shall remove; and nothing shall be impossible unto
you. Matthew 17.19,20.

"Because of your little faith"—Or their unbelief. Such unbelief, we must be careful to notice, comes from believers; therefore it does not refer to not believing the Lord Jesus as Savior. Since the mentioning of the "mustard seed" is metaphorical in character, the mountain must also be metaphorical. The latter speaks of conclusive and deeply rooted dificulties. Although a mountain is most stable, faith has removed many mountains, many difficulties. Unlike wandering stars, mountains sit steadfastly where they are. Matters such as unbelieving children and unemployment are like mountains. Yet faith can remove such mountains and deal with all kinds of difficulties. Why, then, turn first to other people for help?

OCTOBER 5th

After this manner therefore pray ye, Our Father who art
in heaven, Hallowed be thy name. Thy kingdom come.
Matthew 6.9, 10.

"After this manner therefore pray ye"—What follows upon these words was never meant to serve as a prayer form or liturgy for us to say but as an example for us to follow. The disciples are to learn to pray after this manner.

Christians today should take up a monumental responsibility: the bringing in of the kingdom upon the earth through prayer. Why is it that Satan still remains on earth today? Because those who belong to Christ have yet to experience the victory of Christ. "Thy kingdom come"—On the one hand, we may say it is already in our midst; on the other, its appearing still awaits the prayers of the believers.

OCTOBER 6th

He that loveth not his brother whom he hath seen, cannot love God whom he hath not seen. 1 John 4.20.

This is a Bible verse familiar to most people. Note, however, that this verse does not imply that you are to love the brother in your home, it says to love your brother in Christ. Frequently the attitude and action of many people make it impossible for you to love them; nevertheless, if God's love has entered into you, you *will* be able to love them. It is not just loving the brethren whom you love; it is loving the brethren, period! It is not merely loving those brethren who are lovely, but loving *all* the brethren. If you cannot love the brethren, it is proven that there is not the love of the Father in you. If you have the love of God, you cannot help but love the brethren.

OCTOBER 7th

I will give unto thee the keys of the kingdom of heaven.
Matthew 16.19.

That the Lord grants the keys of the kingdom of heaven to Peter confirms the fact that this apostle will do the work of opening doors—first to the Jews and then to the Gentiles. Since the keys of the kingdom of heaven are in Peter's hand, he must of necessity be one who has himself already entered the kingdom of heaven. For the keys are committed to Peter's hand for him to keep. If, for example, the key to the gate has been given into my hand for keeping, people who come early to our meeting will have to wait outside the iron gate till I arrive and open it with the key. I will enter in first and afterwards other people can come in. It is simply impossible for anyone *without* the key to enter first. Hence it is crystal clear that Peter is the first one who enters the realm of the kingdom of heaven.

OCTOBER 8th

But if that evil servant shall say in his heart, My lord tarrieth ... Matthew 24.48.

What is the reason for this servant's faults? "My lord tarrieth"—He truly believes in the second coming of the Lord, except that in his estimation the Lord will come tardily. Whoever does not believe in the soon return of the Lord is an evil servant. What does the Lord say is the fault of this evil servant? Just this, that though he confesses with his mouth that the Lord shall indeed come, he nevertheless says in his heart that the Lord will delay. How precarious is such a position! Will a person watch if he has no idea that the Lord is coming soon? We must have both the attitude and the desire for the soon return of the Lord.

OCTOBER 9th

And the priests that bare the ark of the covenant of Jehovah stood firm on dry ground in the midst of the Jordan; and all Israel passed over on dry ground, until all the nation were passed clean over the Jordan. Joshua 3.17.

The riverbed is the place of death. Nothing at all comfortable, nothing at all appealing. Not restful, not sitting, not lying, but standing. If I live according to my ill-temper, Christ cannot live in others. But if I stand at the bottom of the river, other people will cross the Jordan to victory. Death works in me, but life works in others. In my obedience to death, life will operate in others for their own obedience to God. The death of Christ quickens His life in us. Without death there can be no life.

It was most agonizing to bear the ark at the bottom of the river, for it required great diligence. A slight carelessness and the holy God would destroy them. They stood there, watching the children of Israel pass by one by one. And so they were left to the last. May we be able to pray thus: O Lord, let me die that others may live.

OCTOBER 10th

Exercise thyself unto godliness. 1 Timothy 4.7.

Some Christians mistake rigidity to be godliness. They make themselves false. One brother said he met another brother who would either lower his head towards the ground or lift up his head towards heaven after a word or two. He discovered that this brother was pretending godliness. He wished to shout to him from his heart: "Brother, do not pretend!" We should know what life is: that which flows naturally. With such rigidity in a brother, neither his spirit nor his God is able to come forth. So in exercising ourselves unto godliness we always need to be living and fresh, for it is God who manifests himself through our words and attitudes.

OCTOBER 11th

Now is the judgment of this world: now shall the prince of this world be cast out. John 12.31.

Even though at present Satan temporarily rules over the world, he is but a usurper who has occupied it by force. When the Lord Jesus died on the cross He already cast out the prince of this world. In His death He "despoiled the principalities and the powers . . . [and] made a show of them openly, triumphing over them in it" (Col. 2.15). Although the world still lies under the evil one, it is totally illegal. And God has appointed a day when the kingdom shall be retaken and His Son shall be king over this world for a thousand years, and onward, then, to eternity. Yet before that time arrives God only permits Satan to remain active, while He himself holds the reins of government of this world. Satan may rule over all that belongs to Satan himself, he may even persecute all that belongs to God; nonetheless all of this is but for awhile. And even in this short while, Satan is entirely restricted by God. He may harass the saints but only within certain limits. Aside from what God permits, the enemy has no authority whatsoever.

OCTOBER 12th

Watch therefore: for ye know not on what day your Lord cometh. Matthew 24.42.

What is the significance of the word "watch"? The meaning of watching is not to be careless. How prone Christians are to be overly self-confident. Watchfulness is the very opposite of carelessness. He who sleeps must be so confident in himself that he reckons nothing is going to happen, whereas the watchful person puts no trust in his flesh at all. The self-confident one is prone to fall, for to boast that "I am different from yesterday" opens the way to failure. Only the person who deeply senses his own inadequacy will be watchful. Since the Lord has not told us the hour, let us ever be watchful and on guard.

OCTOBER 13th

Jesus answered and said unto her, If thou knewest the gift of God, and who it is that saith to thee, Give me to drink; thou wouldest have asked of him, and he would have given thee living water. John 4.10.

On the day that the Lord Jesus sat down by the well of Jacob in Samaria He was hungry and thirsty. But the Samaritan woman was more thirsty than the Lord. So He offered living water to her that she might be satisfied. When the disciples came back with the food, He was no longer hungry (see John 4.5–34). From this episode in the life of our Lord we learn this spiritual lesson, that whoever serves others in order that they may not be thirsty shall himself be satisfied: that the one who learns to bear another's burden shall find his own burden easier to bear. In spiritual work, there is no possibility of retirement: "My Father worketh even until now," declared the Lord Jesus, "and I work" (John 5.17).

OCTOBER 14th

And I will take away the stony heart out of your flesh, and I will give you a heart of flesh. Ezekiel 36.26.

The stony heart has reference to the hardness of the heart, while the heart of flesh has reference to a softness or tenderness of heart. On the day a person gets saved his hardened heart is softened, yet we dare not say it is totally softened.

The progress of our life hinges entirely on the transformation of our heart—whether it is hard or soft. If our heart is seized by anything outside of God—be it an event, a person, or a thing—the operation of life will as a rule be hindered. For this reason God will transform our heart continuously until it wholly becomes like tender flesh. Then His Spirit is able to cause our inner life to expand with strength. Just be willing to obey God and His life will move into the conscience, mind, will, and emotion of your heart. It will keep on moving.

OCTOBER 15th

For to me to live is Christ. Philippians 1.21.

God does not make you a Christian in the way a person teaches a monkey how to dress, eat, and move. To teach a monkey to live like a man would be such a burden to it that it would rather remain as it is than learn to be a man.

Jesus Christ is our life to do everything in us. God never demands Christians to *do* this or to *do* that. For Paul says, "For me to live is Christ"—and having Christ living in him, Paul is able to endure beatings, persecutions, many perils, imprisonment in Jerusalem, and transference to Rome. It is not by his being like Christ nor imitating Christ, but by Christ living in him that he finds strength for all such things. As a monkey cannot be transformed into a man, so a Christian cannot imitate Christ.

OCTOBER 16th

Among them that are born of women there hath not arisen a greater than John the Baptist: yet he that is but little in the kingdom of heaven is greater than he. Matthew 11.11.

John is termed greater than all the prophets, yet not in the sense that he surpasses all other prophets in faith, conduct, fame, work, and the Holy Spirit—he is greater only in a specific sense. All the prophets prophesied until John. John himself does not prophesy, however; he merely points out Christ to man: "Behold, the Lamb of God"—it is just here that he is greater, for in time and opportunity he is different from the rest.

"Yet he that is but little in the kingdom of heaven is greater than he"—This does not mean that John's faith, conduct, spiritual life and work are small and that he is therefore unable to enter the kingdom of heaven. It merely signifies how those who are in the kingdom of heaven may testify to the fact that the work of Christ is already done.

OCTOBER 17th

And Solomon . . . came to Jerusalem, and stood before the ark of the covenant of Jehovah, and offered up burnt-offerings, and offered peace-offerings. 1 Kings 3.15.

Before the Lord had appeared to him, Solomon did not realize or sense the significance of the ark; but once he experienced the Lord's appearance, he became aware of the preciousness of the presence of the Lord over and above all other things. With the result that he immediately returned to Jerusalem and offered sacrifices before the ark of Jehovah. In Gibeon, Solomon had only offered burnt-offerings; but now he offered burnt-offerings and peace-offerings and made a feast for all his servants. Oh, to worship before God is true worship, to commune with God is true communion, and to rejoice in God's presence is true joy. This is what Solomon had experienced. And after Solomon had built the holy temple, he placed the ark in it. And the ark became the center of the holy temple.

OCTOBER 18th

Being justified freely by his grace through the redemption that is in Christ Jesus: whom God set forth to be a propitiation, through faith, in his blood. Romans 3.24, 25.

Before Christ came into the world human beings suffered two great losses: first, the loss which came from Adam having sinned; and second, the loss which came from our inability to keep the law of God. With death and sin ruling, we are thus separated from God and cannot enjoy His presence. We become foolish and know not God. We do not possess the spiritual life and power to do God's will. Alas, in Adam and under the law we have nothing whereof to boast except to cry out: "Wretched man that I am! Who shall deliver me out of sin and death?" Is there no way to solve the problems of sin and death? Indeed there is: in shedding His blood, the Lord Jesus has solved both problems. Because of His shed blood we need not die and our sins are being cleansed.

OCTOBER 19th

Much more shall they that receive the abundance of grace and of the gift of righteousness reign in life through the one, even Jesus Christ. Romans 5.17.

Actually we may "reign in life" now, even though the full realization does await the future. Today we may indeed rule over all things by exercising the authority which our Lord has given to us. We should be kings today who rule over all the evil spirits by stopping their works. If Satan will eventually be bound during the millennial kingdom, we can certainly use "the powers of the age to come" (Heb. 6.5) *now* to confine his activities. We may also use today the weapon of prayer to control our circumstances. Whether it is a national, family, church or personal affair, we may govern it by prayer.

OCTOBER 20th

The tree of life also in the midst of the garden. Genesis 2.9.

When the created being lives by his created life, he does not need to be very dependent on God. But for the created being to live by the life of the Creator, he has to be wholly dependent because the life he would then live by is not his but God's. He could not be independent of God but would have to maintain constant fellowship with Him and completely rely on Him. Such life is what Adam does not have in himself and so he must trust God to receive it.

Moreover, such life—if received by Adam—is what he could not live out by his own effort; and therefore he would have to depend on God continuously in order to keep it.

And thus the condition for keeping it would become the same condition for receiving it. Adam would have to depend on God day by day in order for him to live out his godly life in a practical way.

OCTOBER 21st

And having gifts differing according to the grace that was given to us. Romans 12.6.

The portion of service which we have in the body of Christ is based on our knowledge of Him. Yet this is not a common knowledge, because a common knowledge of Christ is inadequate. Only a specific knowledge of Him will constitute a specific ministry in serving the body of Christ. Having learned what others have not learned, you receive from the Lord a specific lesson, and with this specific knowledge of Him you may serve. In the human body, for example, the eyes can see, the ears can hear, and the nose can smell. They have their own functions, and thus each has its own portion. Similarly with the members of the body of Christ. Not every member can see or hear or smell; but each member has his own special ability. This, then, is that member's ministry.

OCTOBER 22nd

I will not leave you desolate [orphans, mg.]: I come unto you. John 14.18.

The Lord will not leave us as orphans. He will himself take care of us, nourishing us, edifying us, and bearing the full responsibility for us. In other words, the in-dwelling Holy Spirit is to translate into our subjective experience the objective fact of what Christ has accomplished for us on the cross. The Spirit of truth is to guide us into reality.

"Comforter" in the Greek original includes two thoughts: one means "called to one's side" — that is, to one's aid. This is to say that the Holy Spirit is our present help. Whenever we need His aid, He is always alongside us to help. The other means "one who pleads another's cause" — an advocate. Christ, as it were, appears before God to plead for us — that is, to plead for our good.

OCTOBER 23rd

Wherefore girding up the loins of your mind, be sober and set your hope perfectly on the grace that is to be brought unto you at the revelation of Jesus Christ. 1 Peter 1.13.

As most of us may know, the dress of the Jews in the olden days hung rather loosely on the body and was without any buttons. Each time a person started to work he had to gird up the loins so as to ease his movement. Our scattered thoughts are like ungirded loins. Yet God can gather up our scattered thoughts as a person girds up his loins. How often our thoughts, though not unclean, are scattered and not focused. In prayer and in the study of God's word, our mind will run wild. Our thoughts may not be bad, but even good and tasteful thoughts are not conceived at the right time. This is because the loins of our mind are too loose and not concentrated. Yet God is well able to restrain our minds and bring our thoughts into focus.

OCTOBER 24th

And [Jesus] went down with them, and came to Nazareth; and he was subject unto them. Luke 2.51.

Once a sister told me that if her husband would permit it, she would leave her three children and go preach the gospel in Tibet. She yearned to have all bonds cut off that she might fly away. This, however, is not the Lord's attitude. He is God, yet He was obedient to His earthly parents and cared for His brothers and sisters in the flesh. How we too ought to learn to be obedient; we should not entertain any improper ambition for ourselves. We should submit joyfully if God uses family or children to limit us. It is wrong for merchants to think of not trading, for students to hope of not studying, for teachers to expect not to teach, and so forth. We shall find rest if like our Lord we are willing to accept all kinds of limitations without struggle.

OCTOBER 25th

And [the other malefactor] said, Jesus, remember me when thou comest in thy kingdom. And he said unto him, Verily I say unto thee, Today shalt thou be with me in Paradise. Luke 23.42, 43.

Can a robber be saved? The world would conclude that a man who has plundered and killed ought to perish, for such a dangerous prisoner should be consigned to the deepest recesses of hell. He deserves the heaviest punishment, since salvation in the eyes of the world is the portion only of the good people of the earth. Who, then, would imagine that a robber for life — one who had violated the law repeatedly—could be saved instantaneously at the time of death? But it is a fact of history that one who had never done good but had only done evil throughout his life was saved immediately upon believing in the Lord Jesus. People may be saved in the twinkling of a moment because they believe in the Lord Jesus. What an incredible story! What a marvelous salvation!

OCTOBER 26th

For our wrestling is not against flesh and blood, but against the principalities, against the powers, against the world-rulers of this darkness, against the spiritual hosts of wickedness in the heavenly places. Ephesians 6.12.

Many people know only the battle between the spirit and the flesh; they do not perceive the conflict that rages between us believers and the evil spirits as described in the sixth chapter of Ephesians. The real spiritual battle is fought between us and Satan with his evil spirits. This battle is joined by all matured believers, for the children of God on earth are frequently attacked by evil spirits. Such attacks sometimes occur in the believers' environment, sometimes in their physical bodies, sometimes in their thoughts, sometimes in their emotions, and sometimes in their spirits.

Too often believers are not aware of being attacked by evil spirits. They do not understand why everything seems to be against them, creating terrible confusion and trouble. They too often take these things as natural, not realizing that frequently they are being supernaturally oppressed by the evil spirits.

OCTOBER 27th

And the number of them that lapped, putting their hand to their mouth, was three hundred men: but all the rest of the people bowed down upon their knees to drink water. Judges 7.6.

Small things frequently reveal our real situation. In those days both the Jews and Arabs travelled with their baggage on their backs. There were therefore two different ways to drink water while on the road: by unloading the baggage and bowing down upon their knees to drink, or by lapping water from their hands for the sake of hurrying up their journey on the road and of guarding against plunderers. Of the ten thousand men left, 9,700 knelt down to drink; only 300 lapped up the water from their hands. All those who bowed to drink were eliminated by God. Only those who drank from their hands were chosen. Whoever has opportunity to indulge and yet refrains from doing so has known the dealing of the cross. Such persons will be used of God. Ever ready to let the cross work in his life, such is the man whom God will use.

OCTOBER 28th

Butter and honey shall he eat, that he may know to refuse the evil, and choose the good. Isaiah 7.15 mg.

Our Lord had butter and honey; therefore, He could choose the good and refuse the evil. It requires great power to be obedient! If God does not fill your heart first, you will not succeed, no matter how you try externally. We need to learn to draw near to God daily and receive from heaven both butter and honey (the grace and love of God), so that day by day we may live on earth choosing the good and refusing the evil.

I speak to you today in this manner because I have a deep sense within me that the return of the Lord is imminent and that the kingdom is at hand. Henceforth, temptations will be greater, dangers will be multiplied, and deceptions will be deepened. Oh do let us notice one thing: that no matter what is placed before us, we shall be able to choose with singleness of heart only because we have received the heavenly butter and honey.

OCTOBER 29th

And Moses said unto God, Behold, when I come unto the children of Israel, and shall say unto them, The God of your fathers hath sent me unto you; and they shall say to me, What is his name? what shall I say unto them?
Exodus 3.13.

By this time Moses had been dealt with by God. He neither assumed nor imagined. He dared not move presumptuously. That is why he asked the Lord in such a manner. He had learned his lesson, a lesson not unlike the one the Lord Jesus himself spoke about: "For I spake not from myself; but the Father that sent me, he hath given me a commandment, what I should say, and what I should speak. And I know that his commandment is life eternal: the things therefore which I speak, even as the Father hath said unto me, so I speak" (John 12.49, 50). How often our words lack the restraint of God. Moses had come to realize that even the words which he spoke must be commanded by the Lord.

OCTOBER 30th

For Christ also pleased not himself; but, as it is written,
The reproaches of them that reproached thee fell upon
me. Romans 15.3.

Our Lord has "despised" and "endured" (Heb.
12.2) for the sake of the joy of the kingdom. How about
us? Have we forsaken anything for the sake of the glory of
the future kingdom? Have we done what we do not want
to do or not done what we do want to do because of God's
reward? If this joy could attract our Lord, why can it not
attract us? Countless believers, both ancient and modern,
have forsaken all to follow the Lord for the sake of the
glory of the kingdom; how about you and me?

OCTOBER 31st

That ye no longer walk as the Gentiles also walk, in the
vanity of their mind. Ephesians 4.17.

Even if we have already known the truth which we
are to preach, we dare not draw it out from our brain and
deliver it to people. Instead, we will humbly prostrate
ourselves before God, asking Him to quicken afresh the
truth we already knew. And thus the truth will be impressed
upon us anew so that what we speak is not merely the
memory of our past experience but is something which we
seem to newly experience in our life. In this way will the
Holy Spirit with His power verify what we preach. It is best
for us to wait before the Lord for a little while before we
ever speak, allowing His word (or sometimes that which we
already knew) to impress itself upon our spirit afresh.

NOVEMBER 1st

Whosoever drinketh of the water that I shall give him shall never thirst; but the water that I shall give him shall become in him a well of water springing up unto eternal life. John 4.14.

Whatever comes from outside is useless in really satisfying anyone. But if a person receives Christ, the latter will become a spring *in* him so that he is daily satisfied. What men lack is *inner* satisfaction.

Once a man went to visit his doctor. He asked his doctor why he felt life was so tasteless and without hope. After he was examined, he was told that there was nothing physically wrong with him. So the man asked if there was any remedy for such depression. The doctor replied: "You should enjoy yourself. Why don't you go see the theatrical play of a certain clown. He has great ability to make people laugh and to be happy." "I am that clown," said the man, "and though I can make other people laugh, I myself cannot laugh." How sad, yet this is only what the world can give—perhaps a few laughs and some temporary joy.

NOVEMBER 2nd

And they shall not teach every man . . . his brother, saying, Know the Lord: for all shall know me, from the least to the greatest of them. Hebrews 8.11.

Sugar and salt look alike. They are both white and fine. But wait until they come to your mouth, and then you know which is sugar and which is salt. To know sugar and salt externally with the eyes is far inferior to knowing internally by tasting them with the tongue. So too is the knowledge of God. The knowledge that comes to us from outside is only ordinary knowledge; the inward knowledge is the sure one. Whenever God gives us a taste of himself inwardly we will have joy unspeakable. "Oh taste and see that Jehovah is good"! (Ps. 34.8) Is it not strange that God may be tasted by us? It is nonetheless true: "For as touching those who were once enlightened and tasted of the heavenly gift . . . and tasted the good word of God, and the powers of the age to come" (Heb. 6.4, 5). This indicates that spiritual things may indeed be tasted. Thank God, the characteristic of the New Covenant is in letting us taste spiritual things, yea, even God himself. Oh what blessing; and how glorious it is. Hallelujah!

NOVEMBER 3rd

And I also say unto thee, that thou art Peter, and upon this rock I will build my church; and the gates of Hades shall not prevail against it. Matthew 16.18.

Many can testify of the numerous times when they encountered difficulties against which faith and prayer did not seem to produce any victorious effect until one day they rose up and declared: "Jesus, You are Lord, You are King, You have trampled the devil under Your feet, and You have destroyed all the works of the enemy!" As soon as this declaration was made, they were strangely strengthened. In this situation, the best prayer is not one of asking; the best prayer is one of declaring: "You Are!" "You Are!" is the church's declaration of faith. The church is not only built on God's revelation but is also built on men's declaration of the revelation they receive. Declaration as a result of revelation is full of spiritual value. It has the spiritual power to shake Hades.

NOVEMBER 4th

Lord, thou deliveredst unto me five talents: lo, I have gained other five talents. His lord said unto him, Well done, good and faithful servant. Matthew 25.20, 21.

The extra five talents earned does not represent success, it instead represents the goodness and faithfulness of the servant. By outward appearance, Stephen (Acts 6, 7) might have seemed to have been a failure, yet in spiritual reality he had done a good and faithful work. So if a cup of cold water is given for Christ's sake (this is faithfulness), it shall be rewarded. To be faithful means to do it for the Lord. For whom do we really work? Oftentimes we seek for success, not realizing that if success is not for the Lord it is but wood, hay, and stubble. The Lord looks for our faithfulness.

NOVEMBER 5th

Oh, Lord, wherewith shall I save Israel? behold, my family is the poorest in Manasseh, and I am the least in my father's house. Judges 6.15.

It is relatively easy to be humble before God; but to be humble before men or to esteem others as more excellent than oneself is extremely difficult. To say I am the least is comparatively easy, but to confess that I am the least in my father's house is not easy. To acknowledge that my father's house is the poorest is not too hard, yet to admit that my father's house is the poorest in Manasseh is most humiliating. He whose face shines and is unconscious of it, though others can see the light of his countenance, is an overcomer. All who look at mirrors in an attempt to see the light on their faces are definitely not overcomers. Although David was anointed, he looked upon himself as a dead dog (1 Sam. 24.14). Overcomers are those who have the reality of, yet not the name of, overcomers.

NOVEMBER 6th

For it is God who worketh in you both to will and to work, for his good pleasure. Philippians 2.13.

There was once a sister whose conscience was so much under accusation that she reckoned she would never want God's will nor would she ever again obey Him. She was in anguish to such an extent that it was as if she were merely waiting to hear the sentence of death. At that very hour, however, she had a prayer within her. She whispered to God: "O God, though I cannot desire after Your will, I beg You to give me this obedience." Strangely, the word of Philippians 2.13 supported her that day. She had now begun to understand that unless God had worked in her heart she would not have been able to pray such a prayer. Since God did work in her to pray this prayer, He most certainly caused her to will and to work for His good pleasure. He had enabled her to obey His will because such is the purpose of His working. She saw it, arose, and was full of joy.

NOVEMBER 7th

And this is the boldness which we have toward him, that, if we ask anything according to his will, he heareth us. 1 John 5.14.

Whenever a believer is in want, he should first inquire: Will such lack affect God? Does He want me to be in need? Or is it His will to supply my need? When you see that God's will *is* to supply your need, you can then ask Him to fulfill His will by supplying what you need. Having come to know His will, you should now pray according to the will of God which you know. You pray that He will fulfill His will. The question is now no longer whether *your need* is met but whether *God's will* is done. Though your prayer today is not much different from that of the past, nonetheless what you now look for is that the Lord's will in this particular personal matter of yours may be done and not that your own need may be supplied.

NOVEMBER 8th

Fear not therefore: ye are of more value than many sparrows. Matthew 10.31.

Even in the smallest matter God is never careless about His children. Once a couple encountered a storm while crossing the sea. The wife was much frightened, but the husband watched the roaring sea with perfect calmness. His attitude so agitated her that she scolded him. The husband therefore took a knife and gestured to kill her. The wife, however, showed no fear. So he asked her why she was not afraid. She answered that it was because the knife was in *his* hand—which thus gave him an opportunity to explain why he was not afraid of the storm, because it was in God the Father's hand.

NOVEMBER 9th

Knowing this, that our old man was crucified with him, that the body of sin might be done away, that so we should no longer be in bondage to sin. Romans 6.6.

If anyone desires to be delivered from the power of sin and not to be in bondage to it, he must overcome his body. In Romans 6.6 the apostle tells us how our Lord delivers us from the tyranny of the body. The Lord Jesus took our old man to the cross with Him, so as to do away with this our body of sin. "Done away" (or "destroyed") in the original Greek means "to render idle, inactive, inoperative, to cause to cease." By what He has accomplished on the cross, the Lord Jesus renders our body of sin inoperative and inactive so that we are no longer in bondage to sin. The body still exists; it is not destroyed in the sense of being annihilated. It simply finds that its lusts which are due to its physiological structure are disabled and withered by the Lord. We all may overcome through the cross.

NOVEMBER 10th

Being darkened in their understanding, alienated from the life of God. Ephesians 4.18.

Originally God had designed to give to us His own life and all things pertaining to godliness. Due to our sin and the death which comes from sin, we became alienated from God, unable to obtain all that belongs to Him. We lost what God had already given and what He had intended yet to give us. But now the blood of the Lord Jesus cleanses us of our sin and restores our relationship with God (Eph. 2.13), so that whatever He has given or will yet give may come to us without any hindrance. Hence the blood of the Lord Jesus not only reconciles us to God, it also gives us God himself.

NOVEMBER 11th

About the fourth watch of the night he cometh unto them, walking on the sea. Mark 6.48.

The Lord is watching to see if we persevere or if we change. He waits to see whether we go forward or go backward. His eyes are upon you and me. He notices every step of our way. And He well knows how great are our temptations and how difficult are our circumstances. Yet He will not let us suffer beyond the fourth watch. At the time of the darkest hour the Lord will come: for has He not already died for us, and has He not ascended to heaven to pray for us, knowing all our trials? But when the sky is *darkest*, He *shall* return.

NOVEMBER 12th

And the tempter came and said unto him, If thou art the Son of God, command that these stones become bread. But he answered and said, It is written, Man shall not live by bread alone ... Matthew 4.3, 4.

"But"—The Lord's answer is exactly opposite to Satan's query. Satan takes one line, but the Lord adopts another line of thought to oppose him. "It is written" is one of His battle weapons. When temptation comes, resisting will not only help to hold ground but will also usually cause the devil to flee. But there are occasions when the situation appears to be a standoff; declaring the word of God at such times will surely make him flee. The word of God is the sword of the Holy Spirit. The battle will be won by wielding it. Yet it is essential to wield it with faith. God's word is like the verdict of the Supreme Court.

NOVEMBER 13th

That they may all be one; even as thou, Father, art in me, and I in thee, that they also may be in us. John 17.21.

Quite simply, oneness is God himself. When all of us set aside the things outside of God and begin to live in Him, then God who is in us becomes the oneness. Oneness is when God has His absolute place in us. Oneness is when He alone is in all, when He fills all. When the children of God are filled with God, they harmonize with one another. As a matter of fact, Satan, in his attempt to effect the disintegration of us as a body, does not need to stir up opinions and strife among us so long as he is able to plant some impurity in us or somethng else which takes the place of

God. As an illustration of this, have you ever noticed how people mix concrete? If there is some clay blended with the sand, the cement will not firmly congeal. Now for Satan to destroy our oneness in the body, he needs to do nothing but spread a little mud—that which is incompatible with the life of God in us—and we as a body shall disintegrate.

We have but one need, which is, to turn inwardly to God and let Him cleanse us and purify us with the cross and the Holy Spirit.

NOVEMBER 14th

I will put my laws into their mind, and on their heart also will I write them. Hebrews 8.10.

Here lies the difference between the New Covenant and the Old. In the Old Covenant the law was placed outside of men, having been written on tables of stone; in the New Covenant it is put into our mind and written on our heart. What is outside and written on tables of stone must be of the letter (2 Cor. 3.6). What, then, is the law which can be put within us and written on our heart? What is the nature of this law? From the word of God we find that the law which can be put into our mind and written on our heart is not of the letter but of life. Each law may not be of life, but every life has its law. The law which God puts in us is the life which He gives us, even "the law of the Spirit of life in Christ Jesus" (Rom.8.2).

NOVEMBER 15th

In nothing be anxious; but in everything by prayer and supplication with thanksgiving let your requests be made known unto God. Philippians 4.6.

Seldom have I seen Christians without anxiety. The vast majority are weighed down with many worries. There was once a mother who had seven sons. She declared, "I am worried to death about every son of mine until they all grow up to be saved." When a brother told her that it was wrong for her to worry—that it actually was a sin to worry—she retorted by saying, "A mother ought to be anxious for her own children. *Not* to worry is sinful." So this brother showed her the words in Philippians 4.6–7. Yet she regarded the anxiety spoken of there as probably not having reference to her kind of anxiety, for according to her thinking, a wife ought to worry about her husband, parents ought to worry about their children, and businessmen ought to be anxious about their business. Let us clearly see, though, that the Bible states categorically: "In *nothing* be anxious"—period!

NOVEMBER 16th

This kind goeth not out save by prayer and fasting. Matthew 17.21 mg.

The Lord shows us here the prayer after faith. We often say that after having faith there is no need to pray again, for all that is required is praise; for if more prayers are offered, faith will be shaken. This certainly is true with regard to asking God. But as towards demons, it is not so. There must be incessant prayer after faith is given. Having received the faith for casting out demons, we should then ask further for its execution. In Luke 18, the widow perseveres in prayer, asking for revenge on her adversary. The adversary, of course, is Satan, whom we must attack by means of prayer throughout our life. Having had faith, there needs to be prayer and fasting. These two are attitudes as well as acts of conduct, which signify dependence on God and self-denial.

NOVEMBER 17th

But the other answered, and rebuking him said, Dost thou not even fear God, seeing thou art in the same condition? Luke 23.40.

We cannot be absolutely certain why this robber who at the beginning railed at the Lord Jesus should suddenly change and believe in Christ. I think, however, that it probably was due to that precious prayer of Christ as recorded in Luke: "Father, forgive them: for they know not what they do" (23.34). These words must have touched his heart. Such mercy, such love, such gentleness, such fullness of grace must have moved his hardened soul, modified his prejudice, and melted his wicked heart. That prayer caused him to know that the One who was crucified was truly the Christ, the Son of God. The Roman cross caused him to rail at Christ; but the cross of Christ caused him to repent and believe in the Savior. Law and punishment cannot save souls; but grace and love will produce tears and repentance in hardened sinners and draw them near to God for mercy.

NOVEMBER 18th

But, lest we cause them to stumble, go thou to the sea, and cast a hook, and take up the fish that first cometh up; and when thou hast opened his mouth, thou shalt find a shekel: that take, and give unto them for me and thee. Matthew 17.27.

"Cause . . . to stumble" — As a matter of principle, anything which touches the person, the holiness, and work of God allows no compromise; there can therefore be no accommodation in such areas. For other matters which are minor, however, we should imitate the Lord here so as not to offend anybody. Here the Lord exhibits great widsom. He is gentle but not weak, humble but not hesitant. How often in many things He makes ground for other people.

"For me and thee" — This is the order. Why not use "us"? Because the Lord can never stand on the same level with us. He is the Firstborn and the only begotten Son; whereas we are but sons. By hiding His glory the Lord pays tribute; in grace He pays tribute for Peter. He can certainly supply our every need.

NOVEMBER 19th

When [Joseph] heard that Archelaus was reigning over Judea in the room of his father Herod, he was afraid to go thither; and being warned of God in a dream, he withdrew into the parts of Galilee. Matthew 2.22.

Concerning God's guidance, this chapter (Matthew 2) mentions the following factors: the knowledge of the Scriptures, the revelation from heaven, the common sense of man, and faith, waiting and obedience.

We need to exercise common sense in the midst of God's guidance. God only charged Joseph to go back to the land of Israel; He had not told him where in the land he should reside. Had Joseph gone through Jerusalem he would have had trouble. His common sense stopped him, thus giving God an opportunity to lead him.

NOVEMBER 20th

I am the vine, ye are the branches. John 15.5.

Once a brother expended great effort in seeking for victory. He acknowledged that in spite of his constant asking, God had not given him victory. One day he read Christ's words in John 15.5: "I am the vine, ye are the branches." Instantly he received light. He knelt and prayed: "I am the most foolish person in the entire world. The victorious life which I seek is actually something I have already possessed. You *are* the branch, Jesus said, and not that you shall become a branch." For many years he asked to be joined to the tree like a branch, not realizing that he was already a branch joined to the tree. Not till then did he receive the revelation of God, and have real faith. Later he said this: "I was defeated, so I sought for victory; but victory never came. But on the day I believed, victory did come."

NOVEMBER 21st

Her sins, which are many, are forgiven; for she loved much: but to whom little is forgiven, the same loveth little. Luke 7.47.

How can we love the Lord? If we remember how our sins were forgiven, we cannot help but love the Lord. The day the cross ever fails to move us, that very day we are fallen. Evan Roberts wept greatly when he realized that he was not moved by the cross; and this went on for several months until God moved him again. But there then followed the great Welsh Revival, the greatest spiritual renewal the world has ever seen.

How did it happen that that woman washed the Lord's feet with her tears, wiped them with her hair, and kissed them with her lips? It was because she remembered how all her sins had been forgiven her. Let us continually stand at the foot of the cross. And even if later we should become spiritually stronger a hundred times more than what we are today, let us always remember how our sins were forgiven us by the Lord.

NOVEMBER 22nd

That through death he might bring to nought him that had the power of death. Hebrews 2.14.

The Lord Jesus was himself baptized in the river Jordan. His having gone down into the waters of baptism signifies death. His coming up out of the water denotes resurrection. He overcomes death through the power of resurrection. The greatest power of Satan, we know, is death itself (see 1 Cor. 15.26). It is as if the Lord challenges

His enemy by saying, Do whatever you can to Me. And Satan indeed does his uttermost. But God has the power of resurrection. Satan aspires to put the Lord to total death, yet the Lord has a life which cannot be touched or held by death. The Lord, as it were, goes through on dry ground! Apart from the Lord's resurrection, there is no power which can overcome death. The life which we receive at the time of regeneration is this very resurrection life. And the power of resurrection life will sweep away all death.

NOVEMBER 23rd

I have fought the good fight, I have finished the course, I have kept the faith. 2 Timothy 4.7.

May we be runners who run the race to the end. Even if during the running we may be wounded — having, from the hands of men, suffered opposition, misunderstanding and rejection — we must stir up our spirit and keep on running for the sake of the Lord Jesus. Who in a race will receive the most applause from men? Will it not be the one who has been wounded but who still keeps on running until he gains the first prize? Therefore, whether we be wounded or suffering or seemingly defeated, it ought not be a problem. It is still best for us to rise up and run. Let us remember that nothing counts while still on the road; only at the end of the course will judgment be rendered. Hence let us not forfeit the race for whatever reason. Let us not grow weary and become faint. On the contrary, we must look away to Jesus and run to the very end.

NOVEMBER 24th

Let the words of my mouth and the meditation of my heart be acceptable in thy sight. Psalm 19.14.

The heart is the principal problem. Whether or not the outward words are correct is not the central issue, nor is it the correctness of outward attitude. The real problem lies in the intent of the heart. The thought and intent of the heart is the issue that must not be neglected. For this reason, David prays to have the meditation of his heart acceptable to God as much as to have the words of his mouth acceptable. His prayer is for God's acceptance of his inward desire. Hence Paul testifies that David is a man after God's heart (Acts 13).

What kind of man is a man after God's own heart? It is the one who allows God to touch his heart. If a person will not allow Him to touch his heart, he can hardly be a man of God's own heart.

NOVEMBER 25th

Take my yoke upon you, and learn of me. Matthew 11.29.

You find rest when you say to God, I will take up the yoke. What God is leading us into today is for us to be willing to take up His yoke in the small things of each day as well as in the big things in life. Some find it hard to labor with their fellow-workers; some sisters find it arduous to live with their in-laws; some employees find it difficult to work with their colleagues; and some students become weary of their relationshp with teachers as well as with other students. These are yokes to bear. You are of course tired of them. You wish you could leave them or that they would leave you. Please understand, however, that this is the yoke which God has given you; this is the portion God has appointed to you. He wants you to submit to such a circumstance because it is the best for you.

NOVEMBER 26th

Therefore said I, Now will the Philistines come down upon me to Gilgal, and I have not entreated the favor of Jehovah: I forced myself, therefore, and offered the burnt-offering. 1 Samuel 13.12.

We know Saul was rejected by God because he was too zealous, too eager to offer sacrifice, too hasty in prayer. How manifold were his reasons for action; nevertheless, God in the meantime had sought for himself a man after His own heart and had appointed him to be prince over His people. The man the Lord desires is not one who is so hasty that he cannot wait. If the choice were left to us, we would undoubtedly incline towards people like Saul; for was he not an unusual man? He stood head and shoulders above all the people. Yet God does not seek for an unusual man, but a man after His own heart. May the aim of our service to the Lord not be so much a desiring to do great things so that we as well as others may be pleased, but may it be a touching of the heart of God in order that *He* may be delighted. Only people such as this will God use. He is looking for such people.

NOVEMBER 27th

If it die, it beareth much fruit. John 12.24.

The fruit which this grain of wheat bears is manifold. Jesus said, *"Much* fruit" — that is to say, many grains. When we are bound up in our own life, we may gain one or two persons by exerting the utmost of our strength (and thus I do not imply here that we absolutely cannot save anyone). But if we die as the grain of wheat dies, we shall gain "much fruit." Wherever we go, and sometimes by merely dropping a word or two, people will be saved or edified. Let us therefore expect to bear much fruit.

NOVEMBER 28th

And it came to pass at the seventh time, when the priests blew the trumpets, Joshua said unto the people, Shout; for Jehovah hath given you the city. Joshua 6.16.

First you must see the riches that are yours in Christ. This is entering the gate of faith. But then upon entering, you must stand into your new position by dealing with whatever temptation comes your way — be it pride or jealousy or whatever. You stand in faith and declare that all these temptations must fall. And fall they will. Hallelujah! The children of Israel surrounded the city of Jericho and shouted the shout of faith that the walls of Jericho would fall. From the human viewpoint, such action was plain foolishness. But as they shouted, the city of Jericho fell.

NOVEMBER 29th

And he made the candlestick of pure gold. Exodus 37.17.

All the things in the holy place were made of gold: they were so shiny that a mere touch by the priest's hand would instantly reveal his finger prints. Now nothing would seem to matter if one had no intention to come to the holy place to serve; but once anyone entered the holy place to serve, his real image would immediately be revealed. He could not help but see his sins and his uncleanness. He had to confess what he really was, because all that was there was holy.

Whenever we serve God, our true image will be exposed. To really know our self we need to know it in our service to God. The more awareness we have of our self life in the performance of divine service the more assurance we will have that we are those who serve God and that the work we do is truly service to Him. Whoever has such consciousness as this is one who truly serves God.

NOVEMBER 30th

The Revelation of Jesus Christ, which God gave to him
to show unto his servants, even the things which must
shortly come to pass. Revelation 1.1.

In recording all the future events found in the book of Revelation, John aims not at our knowing how and when these things will happen but at our recognizing how Jesus Christ shall reign on the throne. That Jesus Christ is King on the throne—that is what the book of Revelation would have us to know. We know Him as the Savior, yet such a knowledge is not enough, because we must also know Him as King. We must know the severity of the Lord as well as the love of the Lord. Let us clearly understand that the purpose of Revelation is to cause us to know more of this Jesus Christ that we may be watchful and prepared till the day we shall see Him face to face.

DECEMBER 1st

For God so loved the world, that he gave his only begotten Son, that whosoever believeth on him should not perish, but have eternal life. John 3.16.

This precious verse raises three points: a great fact, a great condition, and a great consequence. The great fact is, God sent Jesus to atone for men's sins as the Savior of the world. The great condition is, what every man ought to do—which is to say, to believe. The great consequence is actually so good, it is beyond human thought: whoever believes shall not perish but have eternal life. There is no other fact in the world greater or more real than this we have mentioned. The great condition or demand is now put before every man for him to fulfill—to believe in the fact of what God has done and accomplished. That is the one and only condition. The great fact is done by God but the great condition is fulfilled by men. And with the great consequence of not perishing but having eternal life, a person is in possession of salvation.

DECEMBER 2nd

[Jesus] saith unto them, But who say ye that I am? And Simon Peter answered and said, Thou are the Christ, the Son of the living God. Matthew 16.15, 16.

This is what the church is—the voice of Christ which He leaves on earth. God puts the church on earth to declare and to confess Christ. It would be totally unacceptable for Peter merely to say in his heart: "I believe the Lord has power and He reigns. I believe the Lord is glorious." It would not be enough only for Peter to say: "Lord, I believe You in my heart." What the Lord asks is: "Who say ye that I am?" "Ye" here points to the disciples. It is therefore expected of them to do one thing: to speak out with the mouth. We may think that believing in heart is sufficient or praying alone is adequate. But if we see that the church is to stop the gates of Hades, then we shall appreciate how full of life and power and authority is this declaration of who Jesus of Nazareth is.

DECEMBER 3rd

Every one therefore that heareth these words of mine, and doeth them, shall be likened unto a wise man, who built his house upon the rock. Matthew 7.24.

The wise man is he who does the words of the Lord, while the foolish man is one who does not obey them. The rock stands for the words of the Lord, but the sand signifies the ideas of man. To build upon the rock is to do everything according to God's word; to build upon the sand is to do things according to one's own ideas. "The fear of Jehovah is the beginning of wisdom" (Prov. 9.10). It is therefore wise to be simple before God and foolish to rebel against Him. To say "perhaps" or "according to my own opinion" is really being foolish. To do what God says may look like utter foolishness to man but it is real wisdom to God.

DECEMBER 4th

Now faith is assurance of things hoped for, a conviction of things not seen. Hebrews 11.1.

This is a definition of faith given by the Bible. What is "assurance"? In Greek *(hupostasis)* it means "a standing under," a "support." It is that which supports what is above. Books, for example, are placed on a book shelf, and thus the book shelf supports the books. What is the meaning of "conviction"? This word contains the idea of "proof." Thus faith is that which supports the things hoped for, so that our heart may find rest. Faith also proves in us the things not yet seen, so that we may amen from our heart what God has said.

God is faithful. His faithfulness is the guarantee of His promise and covenant. If we do not believe, we will be offending His faithfulness as though He could lie. So whenever we do not believe, we must condemn our unbelief as sin and ask the Lord to take away our evil heart of unbelief.

DECEMBER 5th

And the God of peace shall bruise Satan under your feet shortly. Romans 16.20.

We believers who have been chosen by the Lord should never forget this purpose of our being involved in destroying the works and the power of the devil. Whatever we do, we should not ask if this matter is good or bad, but ask instead if it is *profitable to God* and *destructive to Satan*. We will not do anything if it has no power to affect the kingdom of darkness and to cause damage to the devil.

In all our works we are to judge them not by the apparent result but by the effect they shall have in the spiritual realm as to who will gain and who will lose. This is spiritual warfare that is not to be waged by the efforts of flesh and blood. This is also to be the criterion at the judgment seat on that day; whether a work is to be burned or to stand shall be based on how effective it was in effecting the will of God.

DECEMBER 6th

Go unto my brethren, and say to them, I ascend unto my Father and your Father, and my God and your God. John 20.17.

This tells us that we have both God and a Father. What then is the difference between God as Father and God as God? The Bible shows us that God as Father signifies His relationship with us individually, while God as God denotes His relationship with the entire universe.

Knowing God as Father causes us to cast ourselves upon His bosom, whereas knowing Him as God induces us to prostrate ourselves on the ground in worship. We are God's children, living in His love and happily enjoying all that he has bestowed on us. We are God's people, standing in our place as men worshipping and praising Him. In knowing Him as God we "worship Jehovah in holy array" (Ps. 29.2)! Just as the psalmist sings: "In thy fear will I worship" (5.7). If a person knows God as God, how dare he not fear Him in all things?

DECEMBER 7th

And he saith unto them, It is written, My house shall be called a house of prayer. Matthew 21.13.

When we talk about the prayer of the church we are no less concerned with private prayer nor sense any less the importance of personal prayer. Yet let us see that it is a rule in the kingdom of God that what one person is unable to do in certain respects is to be done through mutual and corporate help. Especially in the matter of prayer, there is the need for mutuality. All who follow the Lord closely frequently see the need of praying with other believers. At times they feel the inadequacy of their own prayer. Particularly in praying for such a colossal subject as the kingdom of God, it requires the strength of the whole church. "My house," says the Lord, "shall be called a house of prayer" (Matt. 21.13). To this we may add, "whose house are we" (Heb 3.6).

DECEMBER 8th

Let both grow together until the harvest: and in the time
of the harvest I will say to the reapers, Gather up first
the tares, and bind them in bundles to burn them; but
gather up the wheat into my barn. Matthew 13.30.

Wheat needs to be dried (it is different from grapes, which need water). It therefore needs sunlight. The yardstick for being reaped is the percentage of moisture remaining. The stalk and root must be completely dried before reaping. Now we are all wheat, yet we all need to be dried, that is to say, to cease seeking the pleasure of the world. "Wheat dries towards earth but ripens towards heaven," one keenly observed. Now sunlight, which in its severity helps wheat to grow and to ripen, represents in a spiritual way the tribulation needed to dry us out from loving the world. How wise is our God in using wheat to represent the saints, the sons of the kingdom. He waits to see if we are ripened before He reaps. The time for the rapture of a believer is in a sense determined by his ripeness.

DECEMBER 9th

Rise and enter into the city, and it shall be told thee what
thou must do. Acts 9.6.

What the Lord meant by this was: I will not tell you what you are to do, but somebody else will do so. The Lord used someone else to tell Paul. This is a revelation of the body of Christ. On the first day of Paul's salvation, the Lord revealed to him the law or principle of the body. Though Paul is to be a vessel mightily used by the Lord, the Lord nevertheless uses other people to help him. Hence let us never think we do not need to depend on others as though we are to get everything directly from God alone. True, this is not meant to teach us to follow other people blindly, but it does admonish us not to entertain such a lofty attitude wherein we believe we by ourselves may receive the word of the Lord and solve all problems singlehandedly.

DECEMBER 10th

For the law of the Spirit of life in Christ Jesus made me free from the law of sin and of death. Romans 8.2.

What is the nature of this law of life? Such a nature will operate spontaneously along certain lines. For instance, the ear will spontaneously hear and the eye will instinctively see without the need of it being forcibly controlled. So too will the tongue taste food, swallowing naturally what is good and spitting out what is bad — all without the need of any conscious effort. What God puts in us is life, and this life is a law by itself.

Let us illustrate this as follows: Suppose you speak to a dead peach tree, saying, "You should have green leaves and red flowers, and at the appointed time bear peaches." You can say this from the beginning of the year to the end and yet get nothing, because it is dead. If it is a live peach tree, though, it will quite naturally sprout, leaf, blossom, and yield fruit without your asking at all. This is called the law of life, for it operates automatically.

DECEMBER 11th

For I, Jehovah, change not. Malachi 3.6.

God never changes, neither does the work of the Lord Jesus know any change, nor does the Holy Spirit ever change. A child in his ignorance thinks that the sun has disappeared on a rainy day. So he asks his father where the sun went. He climbs the stairs to gain a higher view of the sun, but he cannot find it. He may even ascend a watch-tower nearby, yet still he cannot find the sun. In actuality, though, we older ones know that the sun has not changed; it has merely been hidden from view by dark clouds. Now in just the same way, the believer's Sun does not change, only his feeling does: there are dark clouds in his personal sky so that the light of his Sun is screened from view. If a believer lives in his feeling, his sky will often change and be frequently overshadowed by clouds. But if he does not live according to feeling, his sky will suffer no change at all. We ought to live above the dark clouds of feeling.

DECEMBER 12th

By faith Jacob, when he was dying, blessed each of the sons of Joseph; and worshipped, leaning upon the top of his staff. Hebrews 11.21.

God in His word makes a remark here concerning Jacob's staff. Throughout his life—whether it was leaving home or returning home or going to Egypt—Jacob never left his staff behind. This indicates that he spent his entire life as a pilgrim. God was therefore pleased with him.

Hereafter, we too are to live a pilgrim's life, no longer returning to dwell in the world. Do you have a staff in your hand? Which is your expectation—to remain in Egypt or to pass through the wilderness to reach the Promised Land of Canaan? The world in which you live should be but a pathway for you; and when you die it provides for you only a tomb. Apart from these two things—a pathway and a tomb—you have no other relationship with the world.

DECEMBER 13th

For as the body is one, and hath many members, and all the members of the body, being many, are one body: so also is Christ. 1 Corinthians 12.12.

When you read the Gospel according to Matthew, you see one aspect of Christ; in reading the Gospel according to Mark, you discern another side of Christ; in reading the Gospel according to Luke, still another aspect of the holiness of Christ is in view; and reading the Gospel according to John, yet another facet of the glory of Christ is seen. Moreover, if you read Peter's epistles you behold the splendor of Christ; in reading Paul's epistles, there is still another presentation of Christ; and in pursuing the epistles of John, you must confess that his description of the glorious beauty of Christ excels anything that has ever been written. From all this it must be concluded that our Lord is so great that it requires believers of all ages and from all nations to express Him. The body of Christ is where His life is manifested in all of its varied beauty and glory through the body's members.

DECEMBER 14th

[Jesus] answered and said unto them, See ye not all these things? verily I say unto you, There shall not be left here one stone upon another that shall not be thrown down. Matthew 24.2.

What men see are the outward and the temporary, but the Lord with His spiritual insight sees through the visible. In the eyes of men today how very beautiful is the world and how civilized it is in material things. Yet by seeing with the spiritual eye of the Lord, man can recognize the fact that the earth with all its material objects will eventually be burned. Why then should we believers still mind the things of earth? The disciples did not know that, however good the world is, the day shall come when all will be consumed by fire.

DECEMBER 15th

Forasmuch then as Christ suffered in the flesh, arm ye yourselves also with the same mind; for he that hath suffered in the flesh hath ceased from sin. 1 Peter 4.1.

What kind of weapon is this? It is the best weapon: for it is to be armed with the same mind to suffer as Christ had. Whenever you are obedient to God you will be told by people how hard your life will be and how cruel men will treat you. Yet in response you will think of Christ, of how he suffered in the flesh, and that therefore you too must suffer.

This is the way for us to be armed: we come to suffer. Suffering is not only our duty but it is also our office. Suffering is our business and we embrace it most willingly.

Armed with such a weapon as this, you and I can defeat anything. Not being afraid to suffer, but on the contrary a welcoming of it. Not that we draw back in the face of suffering, but that we let it find us.

DECEMBER 16th

Blessed are the pure in heart: for they shall see God.
Matthew 5.8.

"Pure in heart" means a having as one's single objective the glory and the will of God. Such a man seeks nothing but what God may gain. God is the finality as well as the pursuit. Since he looks for only one thing, he therefore only sees one thing: he seeks God, and hence he sees God. "They shall be priests of God and of Christ" (Rev. 20.6). Priests are those who see God. May no one lose this blessing of seeing God.

DECEMBER 17th

He shall even restore it in full, and shall add the fifth part more thereto. Leviticus 6.5.

There is a basic difference between the nature of the sin-offering and that of the trespass-offering (see v.2). The sin-offering is "to propitiate" whereas the trespass-offering is "to restore."

Our sin must be propitiated before God through the blood of His Lamb. Whatever we sin against men, however, needs to be restored and not to be propitiated. If we are unfaithful in a matter of deposit or if we make a gain through improper means, we must restore it to man. If we do not make restoration, we cannot offer a trespass-offering. To be forgiven by God through the blood of the Lord Jesus is truth. But you will lose the communication with God if you, having sinned against men, refuse to make restoration. Whenever you think of what you did, your conscience will be restive. You are therefore not free to commune with God.

DECEMBER 18th

Christ is all, and in all. Colossians 3.11.

Christ Jesus is said to be the author and perfecter of our faith. Our faith originates in Him and also concludes in Him. What we believe is He alone. We ought to set our mind on Him only. Neither holiness, nor victory, nor perfect love, nor baptism with the Holy Spirit, nor zeal in winning souls, nor any spiritual conflict should steal our heart away from Him. From the beginning to the end, it is the Lord Jesus himself. Our faith takes Him as the end as well as the beginning. Aside from Him we look at nothing. Naturally, if we do continually look off to the Lord Jesus, then holiness, victory, and all the rest of these things will indeed be manifested in our lives.

Forgiveness, justification and regeneration are in Christ. Holiness, victory and fullness of the Holy Spirit are likewise in Christ. Christ is everything. He is the Beginning of all beginnings, the End of all ends. In short, our all is in Him.

DECEMBER 19th

For God doth know that in the day ye eat thereof, then your eyes shall be opened, and ye shall be as God, knowing good and evil. Genesis 3.5.

To God, all actions taken outside of Him are sins. "To be like God," for instance, is an excellent desire; but to attempt to do it without listening to God's command and waiting for God's time is sinful in His sight. How often we reckon evil things as sins but good things as righteousness. God, however, reckons things differently. Instead of differentiating good and evil by appearance, He looks into the way a thing is done. No matter how excellent it may appear to the world to be, whatever is done by the believer without seeking God's will, waiting for His time, or depending on His power—such action is sinning in God's sight.

DECEMBER 20th

They offered him wine mingled with myrrh. Mark 15.23.

We are told that this was to anesthetize whatever pains occur during crucifixion. But our Savior received it not. He refused to avoid any such pains. Before he had come into this world, He had already sat down and counted the cost (see Luke 14.28); He loved the sinners of the world so much that He was willing to submit to all their afflictions. He would rather taste death for sinners once for all and *completely*, so that they might receive eternal life. He would take to himself *all* the bitterness that belonged to sinners in order that they might have the joy of His righteousness.

DECEMBER 21st

That no flesh should glory before God. 1 Corinthians
1.29.

What hinders a believer's progress the most in life
and work is his flesh. He is unaware of God's calling him
to deny his entire flesh. He imagines that forsaking sins is
quite enough. He is ignorant of God's equal displeasure
with his own ability, zeal and wisdom in God's work and
his own goodness and power in spiritual life. Whatever we
reckon as good according to the flesh, whatever we plan
and ingeniously arrange by means of the flesh is something
we must deny, deliver up to death, and allow to pass
through judgment according to God. The Lord has no use
for the help of the flesh, neither in spiritual life nor in
spiritual work.

DECEMBER 22nd

*And the Spirit of God moved upon the face of the
waters.* Genesis 1.2.

"Moved" in the original means "novered" or
"brooded" over. This meaning reveals a picture of loving-
kindness and sensitivity. It is the same word used in
Deuteronomy 32.11 in describing a mother eagle with her
eaglets; and how God is the same: "As an eagle that stirreth
up her nest, that fluttereth over her young, he *spread
abroad* his wings, he took them, he bare them on his pin-
ions." May we respond to the love of God! How His heart
does desire after us! And who are we? Nobody but sinners
—nobody but fallen men! Yet He is not angry at us, nor

does He despise or forsake us. He does not consider us as being unworthy for the Holy Spirit to brood over.

DECEMBER 23rd

Behold the birds of heaven, that they sow not, neither do they reap, nor gather into barns; and your heavenly Father feedeth them. Are not ye of much more value than they? Matthew 6.26.

Anyone who asks "Can God?" or "Will God?" reveals his unbelief. How burdensome it is for men to live without faith in God. Our anxiety can only be alleviated through trusting Him. For five days God restored the earth, and then on the sixth day He created man. He prepares everything man needs before He makes him. Too often we imagine we were created on the first day!

If we know how helpless it is to be anxious, then why be anxious at all? If there is help, there is no need to be anxious. If there is no help, it is equally useless to be anxious.

DECEMBER 24th

Watch and pray, that ye enter not into temptation. Matthew 26.41.

We realize that at no time is a Christian attacked more than at the time he is praying. In other situations you can usually talk with people until eleven or twelve o'clock at night or you are able to work until a very late hour; but when at nine o'clock you try to pray, you sense a drag and want to go to sleep. You do not understand why initially you are well, but at the moment you begin to pray, you feel tired.

The explanation for this is that the enemy is hindering you from praying. He wants to cut your line of heavenly communication because he knows the power of prayer. He realizes how prayer will restrict him and how it will bring down power from heaven.

DECEMBER 25th

Now when Jesus was born in Bethlehem of Judea in the days of Herod the king, behold, Wise-men from the east came to Jerusalem, saying, Where is he that is born King of the Jews? for we saw his star in the east. Matthew 2.1, 2.

If people are not hungry, God will not give revelation. The wise men of the East were perhaps those who waited upon and pursued after God. If all we have is only dead knowledge we will be like the Pharisees. Though we may know the word of the Bible, we do not see the light in heaven. The word of the Bible indeed gave them the details about the Savior; but the appearing of the star in heaven caused them to realize the presence of the Savior! Both the star in heaven and the prophecy of Micah (see Micah 5.2) was necessary. The conditions for receiving God's revelation are to wait, and to desire.

DECEMBER 26th

And they went through the region of Phrygia and Galatia, having been forbidden of the Holy Spirit to speak the word in Asia. Acts 16.6.

Oh do let us see that we are *God's* servants. Though He has entrusted His work to us, He nevertheless eserves for himself the authority to direct His servants. For lo recall that at Antioch the Holy Spirit called the Lord's servants to the work, yet Paul and Silas could not go to Asia by their own choice. The authority over the movement of the Lord's servants is forever in the hands of the Holy Spirit. The question lies not in whether there is need in Asia, but whether God has a need in Asia *at that particular time*. How marvelously the book of Acts shows that the Holy Spirit who gives us power to work is also the One who sets the direction and timing of our work. Our responsibility in the work is simply to supply God's current need.

DECEMBER 27th

And Simon answered and said, Master, we toiled all night, and took nothing: but at thy word I will let down the nets. Luke 5.5.

Since God possesses everything and is able to do everything, He must be all. Everything must be done in the power of the Holy Spirit. Some people may think that if man is reduced to zero the word of God will greatly suffer — that everything will cease its progress and fruit will be diminished, if not eradicated altogether. But what we stress is real spiritual work and real spiritual fruit before God.

The work of the Spirit in only five minutes has more

spiritual usefulness than all our labor through the night that gets nothing. Is it not far better to wait for the Lord's command and obtain a netful of fish in but one casting?

DECEMBER 28th

For it is God who worketh in you both to will and to work, for his good pleasure. Philippians 2.13.

A lady once died, and on the tombstone were inscribed her own words: "She did what she could not do!"

Daily we live through impassable days. For us to obtain perfect salvation and live a clean life, it *has* to be the work of God. Many try to imitate Christ, which they will never succeed in doing. Yet because God does it, I can do it. Hold fast to the fact that He works in me. It is not I who work; I only work because God is first working. If I ever attempt to work out the lofty demands of the Bible by myself, I am destined for failure. All I must do is to ask God to work in me till I am willing.

DECEMBER 29th

His lord said unto him, Well done, good and faithful servant: thou hast been faithful over a few things, I will set thee over many things; enter thou into the joy of thy lord. Matthew 25.21.

In spiritual matters we should recognize the fact that "time" is for "eternity"; that the service we render in time is preparation for the service in eternity. God places us in the here and now for the purpose of training us to be useful in eternity. Time is like a school in which we receive spiritual training and education. Whatever spiritual training and education we receive in time makes us truly fit for God's use in eternity. Revelation 22 informs us that we will serve God even in eternity. Today the Lord places us among the children of God in order that we may learn together with them how to serve and thus prepare us all for our eternal service.

DECEMBER 30th

For as in Adam all die, so also in Christ shall all be made alive. 1 Corinthians 15.22.

We should never forget that all of us were sinners because we all were in Adam. Every one born of Adam inherited the nature of Adam. It took no effort when sinners for us to lose our temper, tell a lie, and so forth, since the life, nature and behavior of Adam flowed in us. Now the way of salvation for us was not in God making us good but in His saving us out of Adam and putting us in Christ. So that now, all which is of Christ flows into us. The Bible shows us that as soon as we are in Adam we sin, and that only as we are in Christ do we practice righteousness. May I remind ourselves that lurking in the secret place of many of our hearts lies an error: the thought of expecting God to change us. But God does not and never will do anything in us; instead, He will put us *in Christ*.

DECEMBER 31st

And he laid his right hand upon me, saying, Fear not;
I am the first and the last. Revelation 1.17.

God has made a beginning with this world, yet what will be its end? To this question God himself gives the answer. In the very first chapter of the book of Revelation we have this declaration by the Lord: "I am the first and the last." This is the revelation of Jesus Christ. And in the last chapter of the book He again declares: "I am the Alpha and the Omega, the first and the last, the beginning and the end" (22.13). This too is the revelation of Jesus Christ.

In other words, what God has begun, He will in truth finish; what has not been solved earlier in the Garden of Eden, He will solve later on. His redemption is perfect and complete; and His eternal plan must be accomplished. All the problems which we cannot resolve today, He will definitely solve in the coming day. Thank God, one day Christ will conclude all things because He is the last just as He is the first. This, then, is the revelation of Jesus Christ. God shows us that this One who is the first and the last is indeed the answer to all questions.